MW01194509

THE NIGHT I GOT KILLED*

BY SAMUEL "SY" BRENNER
AS TOLD TO
ABRAHAM J. SHRAGGE

Copyright 2010 Pending
Book and cover design by Elizabeth Figueroa.

All rights reserved.

ISBN: 978-0-557-72856-5

This book or parts thereof may not be reproduced in any form without prior written permission of the authors.

Formerly copyrighted books, "The Night I Got Killed and What I Did later" and "Man of Confidence", were never published. "The Night I Got Killed," supersedes previous books.

See Sy Brenner at www.SyBrenner.com and video at www.YouTube.com/SyBrenner

To Doctor Benjamin Hulley
  Thank you for your care and
thank you for your caring.
  Be happy and healthy!

For Resa,

"You were meant for me."
I wish you could have read the final copy of this book.

Memoir of a young Jewish Army medic imprisoned in a Nazi camp as head of P.O.W. hospital, spy, and Man of Confidence and life time fighter of P.T.S.D..

A WELCOME

This book has taken many years to write. As with most WWII P.O.W.'s, I have blocked out my memories of the war for the past 50+ years. There are as many stories about the war as there are people who served in it, but this one is quite different, as I have not found any other book that deals with what happens to wounded prisoners of war. It is important to know the effects war has on those who serve, no matter what war. The cover of this book is a pencil drawing done by a Polish prisoner, in exchange for three cigarettes.

As the recollections have flooded back, I have realized the gravity of the circumstances that I endured and how those circumstances have colored the rest of my life.

Through the presence and remarkable bravery of some of the people you will meet throughout the pages of this book, I was able to stay alive and appreciate the goodness in everyday people. These include the Righteous Christian (I will never know his name, unfortunately), who saved me and hid my Jewish identity from the Nazis at my capture when everyone thought I was dead. The incomparable valor of Masa Uchimura in the camp hospital, and the fortitude of Polig and Zaig Monjarret, and the unheralded virtue and courage of 'The Lady', kept me determined and strong enough to survive the horrors of being a Jew in a Nazi Prisoner Camp. Alphonse de la Haye was a model of brilliance and cunning. These were all regular people who are unsung heroes because of the unusual environment in which they found themselves. The war pictures were sent to me by Masa, Alphonse, Polig, and Zaig after the war.

As I have gone through the journey to write this book, I must thank the following people who have helped guide my way.

Because of the San Diego X-P.O.W. group, the encouraging staff of the San Diego Veteran's Administration, and Frank Burger, the Commander of the San Diego X-Prisoners of War Chapter, I have been able to unlock the memories.

Julie Lavardiere P.A., has taken care of my needs for twenty years. Did you ever love your doctor? The other doctors and staff at the V.A., I can never thank enough. Linda Gatto-Woitek, Social Worker and P.O.W. Coordinator of the Department of Veterans Affairs, in San Diego, has helped me through the most stressful time in my later life. Reverend William Mahedy, V.A. Chaplain, Retired, has been my mentor and helped me with my Post Traumatic Stress Syndrome. He got me through my roughest years

Richard Pearson of Piqua, Ohio gave me the original information from the Army and the 2nd Battalion. He was shocked to hear from me, as he said, "You were supposed have been killed on November 29, 1944." Richard was able to corroborate my memories prior to my capture.

Professor Lawrence Baron, from San Diego State University, gave me the locations I should return to in Southern France and Germany. He also helped me with contacting the proper authorities in Europe.

Roland Prieur, the Supervisor of the Cemetery at Epinal, France through the American Embassy, was a warm and vigilant caretaker of the American Cemetery. In 1995, he helped me trace Alphonse de la Hay, and others, only to find they were deceased. He has continued to be a valued friend.

Liz Figueroa who handled the final layout and design of the book, as well as preparing all of the old documents and photographs for use in this book.

Paula Reuben gave me the original push and realities of writing a book.

Don Harrison helped with his contacts for someone to help with the writing and encouragement.

I want to thank my cousin, Melvin Wachs, of Washington D.C. who escorted us and helped us get certain records declassified.

One of my main regrets has been that my parents and siblings never knew what had happened. I have been so touched by the support and love their children and grandchildren have given me.

My sister-in-law and brother-in-law, Lois and Morey Sein accompanied my wife Resa and me on the journey back to Europe, and were there to drive, take pictures and hold me up through the difficult emotional trip back. They are my family and my friends.

My great niece Stephanie Newman for her editing assistance.

Professor Abraham Shragge of University of California, San Diego, was there from the beginning, when he had me come and talk to his classes. He put up with me as I told him my story , and he was able to capture and bring my history to life. His assistance has been invaluable. His student assistant, Mariana Sanchez, brought renewed excitement to this project.

My grandchildren, Bill, Alicia, Seth, Megan, Dylan and Sara bring me such joy and love.

I thank my loving daughter, Donna Cohen, for editing my original book and following through with encouragement in finishing this book and in helping me with the task of getting it published. Thanks, Donna, for being my right hand.

My son Ron Brenner has been there helping with schlepping me and being a great sounding board and friend. Ron helped me to start rewriting the book, and his encouragement deserves special praise and thanks.

My daughter, Mo Bailey was there at the beginning of the recall of memories. She also helps me with my marketing, publicity, and custom created my web site at (www.sybrenner. com).

At 3:35 p.m., on March 14, 2010, my wife Resa, passed away. For almost 61 years she made me happy with love and devotion. Every time we heard "our song", "You Were Meant for Me", she would hold my hand. An avid reader, my regret is that she didn't live long enough to read this book. It is at a time like this that you find your three loving children are your three best friends.

I love you all.

Samuel "Sy" Brenner

January 2010

Samuel "Sy" Brenner

Table of Contents

I was awakened again by a nightmare.
In this dream I saw a German lying there.
He couldn't have been more than sixteen years old. I
touched him to see if he was still alive. He rolled over
and his skull fell open.
I threw up.

I have seen this incident in my dreams at least once or
twice a week for the last sixty years; one of four terrors
that haunt my sleep relentlessly.

These nightmares bring to life actual events I
experienced during World War II.
I have never understood: Why do I never dream about
the night I got killed?

CHAPTER 1

Detroit, Michigan

June 2, 1942

My 20th birthday. A letter from President Roosevelt. "GREETINGS," said the letter from the White House. I was to report for a physical examination. Gee! I was drafted!

Fortunately, I didn't have to show up for my pre-induction physical for several months. When that day finally arrived, I went to this beautiful building in downtown Detroit at the appointed time and was ushered into a long hallway and found that I was standing in line with what seemed to be hundreds of young men. We were handed papers to fill out, and split into two lines, one on each side of the hall. We were then told to take off all of our clothes, including our underwear, and pile them where we were standing. I know I was not the only one who felt ridiculous.

We filed, with forms in hand, into the next room, which was enormous. It actually was a beautiful room, which I imagined must have been a ballroom. It was freezing and the floors were cold. The walls were lined with marble benches. I remember thinking, I was not going to put my ass on that cold marble bench, but it seems like there was an officer nearby who could read my mind and he commanded me to sit my cold ass on that cold slab. It occurred to me, if they took my temperature with a rectal thermometer, I would be pronounced dead on the spot! This is when, at the age of 20, I discovered that Abe Lincoln had never been in the service. If he had been in the service, he would have realized right then and there, like I did, that not all men were created equal. It was also a revelation that I could tell how many Jewish men were in the lines. We were sent from one doctor to the next, each one with his own specialty exams, each one signing a form. It was like a production line.

There were also medics with large syringes, and even longer needles, grabbing each arm as you walked up. One would say to the other, "you use the corkscrew needle, and I will use the square one." I was amazed how many men passed out. They had shots for every kind of disease you could think of but nothing for warming up frozen bodies.

After finishing with all the doctors, we were finally allowed to put our clothes on to our shivering bodies and go to another room lined with many desks, where we turned in all the forms the doctors had filled out. Without looking up, the man at the desk stamped my form 1-A and said, "You are in the Army now."

I was to report to the railroad station in two weeks. I was the first of my group of friends to go into the service. We were a very close group, many of us having been friends since the lower grades of Alger Elementary School in Detroit. Those of us still alive remain friends today. The boys planned a big going away party for me on the night before I left, at one of the nicer restaurants. My best friend, big Bernie Trubowitz, (6'4" tall), and I were known as Mutt and Jeff, as in the comics. We were always together and we always had bets going that we could outdo each other, such as how many ice cream sundaes we could eat at one time or how many corned beef sandwiches we could devour at one sitting. We were very close to each other as well as the guys in our group. When we got into our teen years, we formed a club, calling it the Algonquin Club. Like so many boys at that time, we had weenie roasts, went bike riding and swimming, and took hayrides with our dates. We were a very active social group who cared for each other and for each other's families.

The day before I was to report, my sister Fanny insisted that I come to her house for a steak dinner and she was going to make all the things I loved. I told her that Bernie was going to pick me up and the boys were making me a party, but she insisted. She invited Bernie to come and join the rest of the family and would you believe, we ate that steak dinner at 4:00 p.m. At 7:00 p.m. We were at a nightclub having another steak dinner. Everyone knew I loved steak. We had a great time that night. The fellows gave me a suitcase with my initials on it as a going away present. I had never owned a suitcase before and I really loved it but I said to myself, "What the hell am I going to do with a suitcase?"

My mother and father came to the railroad station to see me off. My brother Saul drove them down for a tearful send off. It was very rough on my mother, as my other brother Myer enlisted the day after Pearl Harbor and was in Pearl Harbor the following week. We hadn't seen him since he left.

I told my mom not to cry but she kept sobbing, saying, "I know, It's "Beshert"." "Beshert" is a Yiddish word that means "it was meant to be."

I was inducted into the Army on December 5, 1942 and was sent to Fort Custer, near Battle Creek, Michigan, where I was processed and given a uniform and other supplies. We were given aptitude tests to see what we were best suited for. Later on during my time in the service, I wondered if anyone ever really looked at the results of the tests as many men seemed totally inappropriate for the jobs they held.

The next thing I knew, we were on a train headed for basic training. This was the first time I had been away from home. I was thrilled at the chance to see the country on a long train ride. I didn't realize that we were headed to the hellhole of the country, Camp Claiborne, Louisiana.

**Following images are film copies of the official
Report of Physical Examination and Induction.**

Armed Forces' Original
D. S. S. Form 221
January 30, 1942

REPORT OF
PHYSICAL EXAMINATION AND INDUCTION

First examination ☒   Second examination ☐   Third examination ☐   Fourth examination ☐
(To be filled in by local board clerk. Check number of examination made by local board.)

(LOCAL BOARD DATE STAMP WITH CODE)

SECTION I.—GENERAL (To be filled in by local board clerk from the Selective Service Questionnaire, D. S. S. Form 40. Write "none" opposite the questions where no information is given. Do not leave any question blank.)

(To be filled in by Armed Forces)

(Armed Forces Serial No.)

	Do Not Enter Anything in This Column
1. Name (page 1) ..Samuel.. ..Seymour.. ..Brenner.. (First) (Middle) (Last)	RESIDENCE State
2. Address (page 1) .3011 Tuxedo.. ..Detroit.. ..Wayne.. ..Mich.. (Street or rural route) (Town or city) (County) (State)	County
3. Social Security No. (Series I, line 5) .... 4. Registrant's order number (page 1) ..12,213..	Place Inducted
5. Physical or mental defects or diseases (Series II, line 1) ..none..	
6. Treatment at an institution, sanitarium, or asylum (Series II, line 2) ..no.. (Yes or no)	DATE INDUCTED
7. Education (Number years completed) (Series III): Elementary school ..9.. High school ..3.. Vocational school, college, or university ..1..	Day
8. Occupation: (a) Title of present job (Series IV, line 2 (a), or Series V, line 1) ..salesman & stockman..	Month
(b) Duties (Series IV, line 2 (b)) ..I sell and am in charge of department's stock..	Year
(c) Title of last job, if unemployed (Series IV, line 3)..	Source
9. Years experience in this work (Series IV, line 2 (e), or Series V, line 2) .2 yr..	Nativity
10. Income (Series IV, line 2 (d)): Average ..weekly.. earnings $ ..20.00.. (Weekly, monthly, annual)	Place of birth
11. Employment class (Series IV, line 2 (c)): Permanent employee ☒; Temporary employee ☐; Apprentice ☐; Independent worker ☐. Unpaid family worker ☐; Employer ☐; Student (Series IV, line 4 (a)) ☐	Race-citizenship
12. Business of present employer (Series IV, line 2 (g)) ..Ernst Kern Co..	
13. Marital status (Series VII, line 1): Single ☒ Widower ☐; Divorced ☐; Married, not separated ☐; Married, separated ☐	Education
14. Number of dependents (Series VII, line 3 (a) fifth column except N. C.'s plus line 4 (a) fifth column) ..2..	Occupation
15. Birthplace (Series IX, line 1) ..Montreal.. ..Quebec.. ..Canada.. (Town or city) (State) (Country)	Marital
16. Birth date (Series IX, line 2) ..June.. ..2.. ..1922.. (Month) (Day) (Year)	
17. Race (Series IX, line 3): White ☒; Negro ☐; Other (specify) ...	
18. Citizenship: United States citizen (Series IX, line 4) ..no.. ; Declarant alien (Series IX, line 7) ..yes.. (Yes or no) (Yes or no)	
19. Previous U. S. military service (Series XII): None ☒; Army ☐; National Guard ☐; Navy ☐; Marine Corps ☐; Coast Guard ☐	
20. Type of discharge (Series XII): Specify ...	
21. Date of registrant's affidavit (top of page 8) ..11th.. ..Sept.. ..1942.. (Day) (Month) (Year)	

INSTRUCTIONS

1. An original and three copies of this form will be prepared for each registrant called up for physical examination. The original is designated as the Armed Forces' Original; the first carbon copy, the National Headquarters' Copy; the second carbon copy, the Surgeon General's (Army)—Bureau of Medicine and Surgery (Navy)—Commandant Marine Corps (M. C.) Copy; and the third carbon copy, the Local Board's Copy.   Instructions are contained on each copy.

2. Forms of men rejected by the armed forces will be marked "Rejected by the Armed Forces" in large letters at the top of page 1.

3. If the registrant is not sent to the induction station of the armed forces, or is rejected by the induction station of the armed forces, this original will be filed, along with "Local Board's Copy" (3d copy), in the registrant's Cover Sheet (Form 53).

4. For registrants accepted by the induction station of the armed forces: If inducted by the Army, this original accompanied by F. B. I. Military Fingerprint Card will be forwarded from induction station to The Adjutant General, Washington, D. C.; if inducted by the Navy or Coast Guard, this original will be forwarded through the Main Recruiting Station to the Bureau of Navigation, Washington, D. C.; if inducted by the Marine Corps, this original will be sent to the Commandant, Headquarters, U. S. Marine Corps, Washington, D. C.

5. Fingerprints are required only on this original and only for registrants who are inducted. If inducted by Army, prepare F. B. I. Military Fingerprint Card.

16—20941-1

ORIGINAL COPY   (PAGE 1)   6731

Section II.—REPORT OF LOCAL BOARD EXAMINING PHYSICIAN AND LOCAL BOARD CLASSIFICATION.

If registrant's answer to Item 6 above is "yes," when and for what ailment(s) ......

Is registrant now or previously an enrollee in the Civilian Conservation Corps: No ☒; Yes ☐
Serological test (syphilis): Date 10-15-4... Result ......
Second serological test (syphilis): Date ...... Result ......
Examining physician's remarks ......

Do you find that the above-named registrant has any of the defects set forth in Part I of the List of Defects (Form 220)?
(If in doubt, answer "no," and give details.) ...... If answer is "yes," describe the defects, in order of significance.

Do you find that the above-named registrant has any of the defects set forth in Part II of the List of Defects (Form 220)?
(If in doubt, answer "no," and give details.) ...... If answer is "yes," describe the defects, in order of significance.

(c) I have examined the above-named registrant in accordance with Selective Service Regulations.
(d) Signature of examining physician ......
(e) Place ...... Wayne ...... (f) Date ......

27. (a) This Local Board has classified the above-named registrant in Class ......
(b) Signature of Member of Local Board ......
(c) Place ...... (d) Date ......

Section III.—NEAREST RELATIVE, PERSON TO BE NOTIFIED IN CASE OF EMERGENCY, AND DESIGNATION OF BENEFICIARY (To be filled out at the induction station for only those registrants accepted for military service)
A. Nearest relative and person to be notified in case of emergency:
28. Nearest relative ...... Rebecca Brenner
(Other than wife or minor child. Name in full)
29. Relationship ...... mother 30. Address ...... 3911 Tuxedo ...... Detroit, Michigan
31. Person to be notified in case of emergency ...... same
32. Relationship ...... 33. Address ......
B. Designation of beneficiary:
34. The persons eligible to be my beneficiary are designated below:
(1) ...... None
(2) ...... None
35. In the event of my leaving no widow or child, or their decease before payment is made, I then designate as my beneficiary the dependent relative whose name, relationship, and address are shown below:
(3) ...... Rebecca Brenner (mother) same as above
36. In the event of the death or disqualification of the last-named dependent relative before payment is made, I then designate as my beneficiary the dependent relative whose name, relationship, and address are shown below:
(4) ...... Morris Brenner (father) same as mother's
37. Signature of registrant ......
38. Witnessed at ...... Detroit, Michigan ...... on ...... November 24, ... 1942
...... J.F. Faso ...... 1st Lt., Inf.

ORIGINAL COPY (Page 2)

Section IV.—PHYSICAL EXAMINATION RESULTS: (All Items Must Be Filled In. Indicate Normal or None Where Applicable.
To Be Filled at by the Medical Board at the Induction Station of the Armed Forces.)

		Do Not Write In This Column
39. Eye abnormalities ...... None	60. Vision, without correction:	
40. Ear, nose, throat abnormalities ...... None	(a) Right eye 20/30	
	(b) Left eye 20/20	
41. Mouth and gum abnormalities ...... None	61. Vision, with correction:	
	(a) Right eye	
	(b) Left eye	
42. Teeth: (a) Indicate restorable carious teeth by circling; nonrestorable carious	62. Color perception:	

SECTION IV.—PHYSICAL EXAMINATION RESULTS: (All Items Must Be Filled In. Indicate Normal or None Where Applicable. To Be Filled Out by the Medical Board at the Induction Station of the Armed Forces.)

Do Not Write in This Column

39. Eye abnormalities ... None

40. Ear, nose, throat abnormalities ... None

41. Mouth and gum abnormalities ... None

42. Teeth: (a) Indicate restorable carious teeth by circling; nonrestorable carious teeth by /; missing natural teeth by X.

Right   EXAMINEE'S   Left
8 7 6 5 4 3 2 1   1 2 3 4 5 6 7 8
16 15 14 13 12 11 10 9   9 10 11 12 13 14 15 16

(b) Remarks, including other defects ... None

(c) Prosthetic dental appliances ... None

(d) Remediable dental defects ... None

43. Skin ... Normal
44. Varicose veins ... None
45. Hernia ... None
46. Hemorrhoids ... None
47. Genito-urinary (non-venereal) ... Normal
48. Venereal diseases ... None
49. Feet ... Normal
50. Musculoskeletal defects ... None
51. Abdominal viscera ... Normal
52. Cardiovascular system ... Normal
53. Lungs ... Normal
54. Chest X-ray ... X-RAY OF CHEST NEGATIVE
55. Mental ... Normal
56. Nervous system ... Normal
57. Endocrine system ... Normal
58. Other defects and/or diseases or other remarks ... None

59. Summary of defects in order of significance ACCEPTABLE UNDER MR 1-9

60. Vision, without correction:
   (a) Right eye ... 20/30
   (b) Left eye ... 20/20
61. Vision, with correction:
   (a) Right eye ...
   (b) Left eye ...
62. Color perception* ...
63. Hearing:
   (a) Right ear ... 20/20
   (b) Left ear ... 20/20
64. Height ... 65 inches.
65. Weight ... 135 pounds.
66. (a) Girth, at nipples; inspiration ... 36 inches.
   (b) Girth, at nipples; expiration ... 34 inches.
   (c) Girth, at umbilicus ... 30 inches.
67. Posture:
   Good ☒ Fair ☐ Poor ☐
68. Frame:
   Heavy ☐ Med. ☒ Light ☐
69. Color of hair ... brown
70. Color of eyes ... hazel
71. Complexion ... ruddy
72. Pulse, sitting ... 72
73. Pulse, after exercise* ...
74. Pulse, 2 minutes after exercise* ...
75. Blood pressure:
   (a) Systolic ... 110
   (b) Diastolic ... 80
76. Urinalysis:
   (a) Specific gravity ... 1.012
   (b) Albumin ... neg
   (c) Sugar ... neg
   (d) Microscopic* ...
77. Other data:

* When indicated.

ORIGINAL COPY   (PAGE 3)   6731

tion IV.—PHYSICAL EXAMINATION RESULTS—Continued.

I certify that the above-named registrant was carefully examined, that the results of the examination have been correctly recorded on this form and that to the best of my knowledge and belief—

(a) ___SAMUEL SEYMOUR BRENNER___ is physically and mentally qualified for general military service.
(Enter name of registrant if this subsection is applicable)

(b) _____ is physically and mentally qualified for general military service after the satisfactory correction of the following remediable defects: _____
(Enter name of registrant if this subsection is applicable)

_____

This registrant would have been accepted for general military service had the remediable defects herein specified been remedied at the time of this examination.

(c) _____ is physically qualified for limited military service only by
(Enter name of registrant if this subsection is applicable)
reason of _____

_____

(d) _____ is physically qualified for limited military service after the
(Enter name of registrant if this subsection is applicable)
satisfactory correction of the following remediable defects: _____

_____

This registrant would have been acceptable for limited military service had the remediable defects herein specified been remedied at the time of this examination.

(e) _____ is physically and/or mentally disqualified for military service by reason of
(Enter name of registrant if this subsection is applicable)

_____

(f) _____ is disqualified for military service because of _____
(Enter name of registrant if this subsection is applicable)

_____

(g) Signature _____ (h) Title _____
Medical Examiner

(i) Name typed or stamped ___MORRIS B. S...___

(a) ___SAMUEL SEYMOUR BRENNER___ was this date inducted for (general; ~~naval~~) [strike out inapplicable
(Enter name of registrant if this subsection is applicable)
word] military service into the (fill in appropriate Service, such as Army, Navy, Marine Corps, or Coast Guard) _____
___ARMY___ of the United States and ~~XXXXX~~ Transferred to ERC to report on Dec. 5,
1942 for Duty North Shelter, Michigan

(b) _____ reported for service in the fill-in appropriate
(Enter name of registrant if this subsection is applicable)
service, such as Army, Navy, Marine Corps, or Coast Guard) _____ of the United States.

(c) Place ___Detroit, Michigan___ (d) Signature _____
(e) Date ___Nov. 24, 1942___ (f) Name typed or stamped ___J.P.Pass___ ___1st Lt., Inf.___
(Grade and organization)

SECTION V.—LOCAL BOARD CHANGE IN CLASSIFICATION AFTER EXAMINATION BY THE INDUCTION STATION OF THE ARMED FORCES.

(a) Based on the entries in (a), (c), (d), (e), or (f) of Item 78, above, the Local Board has changed the above-named registrant's classification to Class _____
(b) Based on the entries in (b) of Item 78, above, the Local Board has retained the above-named registrant in Class _____
(c) Place _____ (d) Date _____
(e) Signature of member of local board _____

FINGERPRINTS—RIGHT HAND

1. THUMB	2. INDEX	3. MIDDLE	4. RING	5. LITTLE

ORIGINAL COPY   (PAGE 4)

They never told us we would be haunted in the years following the war.
Nightmare after nightmare, the war remains alive in our minds.
My memories of the battlefield are very vivid: men wounded, men dying, men having their arms and legs blown off in the heat of battle.

CHAPTER 2

Camp Claiborne Louisiana

December 4, 1942

We were deep in the swamps near Alexandria. The train moved slowly through the camp, periodically making stops as the cars emptied out along the way. Out of the windows of the train, we saw rows and rows of dusty tarpaper barracks. Overall, about 13,000 guys came from all over the Midwest. We were supposed to be "filler replacements," whatever that meant. I wonder, had we known we would be replacing soldiers who had been killed or wounded in battle, would that have curbed our enthusiasm?

We were told to get out and were left standing in a group as the train moved on. Two of the guys were from Detroit like I was, Pat White and another guy called Chris. His real name was Irvin Chrzanowski, but in the Army, you rarely used a guy's first name. The sergeant always used the last name or a nickname if he couldn't pronounce someone's last name. The names seemed to stick. My name is Sam, but my family and friends have always called me Sy. The sergeant called me Brenner, and that is what everyone called me for the rest of the time I was in the service.

There was a group of guys from Chicago, Jack O'Callaghan, Carl Martin, Vincent Petraitis, and Bob Johnson. Mark Gauvin was from Oklahoma. I never figured out how a kid from Oklahoma got in our group, but he was welcome just the same. We each came into the Army alone, but now, simply because we were standing together next to the tracks, we were suddenly friends. So this was the 103rd Infantry, 410th Regiment, Second Battalion.

We learned very quickly why it was called, the "Cactus Division", -because the officers and noncoms were so prickly, in fact, we wore cactus patches. We were greeted by Sergeant Alfred Neimeyer who had us stand in a line. He walked up and down in front of us saying that he had never seen such a bunch of fuck-ups in all his years in the Army. "Any man fucks up in this platoon and I'll have all of your civilian asses." I didn't even know what a platoon was. After that, things started to happen very quickly. We were led into our tarpaper barracks and immediately taught to make up our bunks the GI (Government Issue) way.

We each were issued a M1 Garand rifle, taught how to take it apart and put it back together again. We even had to do it blindfolded. After that, we were shown where (and what) the latrine was. We were amazed when we saw some thirty toilets lined up with no partitions, as well as many urinals. The shower room was also very large. It was in the shower that I first saw scrawled on the wall the notice that "Kilroy was here." Kilroy seemed to have been everywhere I went in the Army. I learned a lot of other new expressions like, "hubba-hubba" and "snafu" which meant, "Situation Normal, All Fucked Up."

As the day progressed, many men were added to our unit, guys from all over the country. Some were much older, twenty-five to thirty years of age. They were a part of the service company of the 2nd Battalion. Most of these men were truck drivers and mechanics, and that is how the service company was rounding out as specialists. The service company provided the Battalion with all its basic needs: Food, motor pool, truck drivers, mechanics, social services, Chaplains and all types of maintenance. In the end, there were twenty-five men in the barracks.

Mail call was always a very important time for all of us, being away from home. It was rough on the guys who couldn't read or write and there were a lot of them, especially those from the South. Some of us read their mail for them and wrote their letters.

There was always some inspection going on. The barracks was inspected. Your rifle was inspected. If you didn't pass the inspection, you got extra duties and when you were done with the extra duties, you were inspected again. K.P. (kitchen police) was a frequent result of not passing an inspection. Some guys had to clean the latrines with a toothbrush. The area around the barracks also had to be kept clean. This was called, "Policing the area," and though Kilroy seemed to have been in the area, he didn't police the area, so we had to do that ourselves.

Some of the inspections were real eye-openers. We had regular "short arm" inspections. We were all lined up in the nude, wearing only our raincoats. When the medical officer walked by, the raincoat was opened and the man had to pull back the foreskin of his penis to show that he was clean and didn't have any form of a venereal disease. Being Jewish and not having a foreskin was helpful in this case, especially since guys with problems had to have their foreskin removed. Just the thought makes me squirm. It was one of the few advantages of being a Jew in the Army. There weren't many pluses in that regard.

There were, however, many negatives. There was a very popular fire-breather named Father Coughlin who preached anti-Semitism every Sunday on the radio. People like Father Coughlin and even the famous industrialist Henry Ford, were a few well-known voices of anti-Semitism. Though I had heard Father Coughlin's sermons and knew very clearly what Henry Ford believed about the Jews, basic training was the first place I had personally encountered anti-Semitism.

I never did find out how Chris knew I was a Jew. I didn't try to hide the fact, but I didn't exactly draw attention to it either. He'd been giving me the business about it for a few weeks.

There wasn't much to do at night except go to the Post Exchange, known as the P.X., or watch a movie once a week. Occasionally we had a friendly game of poker, which I enjoyed very much. One evening, in the middle of the game, Chris looked at me and, for no apparent reason, said, "OK 'Jew Boy', put your money in, you fucking kike."

No sooner than the last word was said, I was on my feet with fire in my eyes, ready to fight. Before that night, no one had ever told me they had trouble with my religion. I felt both of my arms restrained by Pat and Arvel Gullege. Chris's best friends, Martin and Petraitis, dragged him away from the table, telling him to keep his fucking mouth closed or he'd have trouble. From that night on, Chris and I made very little eye contact and had very little to do with each other, unless it was in the line of duty.

We worked in a supply unit and received reports from each company, each day, showing their strength in the men of the 2nd Battalion. We would then ration out and deliver the food accordingly. It was a great job as Army jobs go. It called for a sergeant's rating, but all ratings were frozen because there were nineteen old master sergeants assigned to our company from Panama, waiting to be discharged because they were too old to stay in the service.

My best buddy during basic training was Pat White. Pat was about two inches taller than I with very dark features and a square cut jaw. Both of us coming from Detroit, we had a lot in common. We both loved the Tigers. He used to call me an old reprobate, even though he was actually older than I was and a lot more experienced in many ways. There were two things that stand out in my memory of Pat. First, he was a smoker and I used to watch him strip down his used cigarettes and let the tobacco blow in the air so they wouldn't cause a litter problem. Second was that he must have been quite a ladies' man. He used to tell me stories about how, before the war, he worked at a White Castle Hamburger joint that was so small it only had ten stools in it and the hamburgers were only a nickel apiece. Still, it was big enough for Pat to get laid on the toilet in the rest room. He was always telling me stories like that and as I got to know him more and more I realized they were probably true. I really appreciated Pat's company and was glad later on, after basic, when we were transferred together to Medic Training.

Being in the service company, we ate better than the average man. There were many times I was invited to another company's mess hall by the mess sergeant and ate steak, while the others were eating stew. This was very good for me because being Jewish, I wouldn't eat pork and many times had to live on Hershey Bars.

We worked out of a warehouse called "S4," from where we distributed the food. It was also the headquarters for all other supplies. Anything anyone needed was in S4. It was a large building with a high ceiling. One time one of the men had to climb all the way to the ceiling to get a can of rust-colored paint used to paint rain gutters. The can slipped out of his hand and I watched it fall, landing on the lip, opening the can slightly. As the reddish paint oozed out onto the floor, he just stared at it, saying, "Lay there and bleed to death." Ever since that day, I say the same words whenever I see something fall like that. One of the guys dipped his finger into the paint and with his finger spelled, "Kilroy was here" on the wall.

We were usually finished with our work by 11:00 a.m. and would have a chance to get cleaned up and rest a little before lunch. After lunch each day, we had our infantry training.

We trained pretty hard. For the most part, basic training was a miserable experience. We were sure that all our training in that hot, muggy climate meant we were headed for the Pacific. Twenty-five mile hikes through the swamp were common. We had a Battalion colonel named Selk who loved to take those twenty-five mile hikes. He would run up and down the line yelling, "Only ten more miles, men." He would yell this again after the next ten miles. I heard that he had been a first baseman in the New York Giants minor league system before the war.

Along with the climate came the snakes-the rattlesnakes and the small, beautiful red and black coral snakes. They were the deadliest of all and caused many snakebite casualties. We were also covered with bites by chiggers, little red insects that crawled under your skin and chewed away. The only way you could really get rid of them was to light a cigarette and apply it as close to your skin as possible, until it came out. I still have a prescription excusing me from wearing leggings for three days, thanks to the fact that my legs were nothing but a mass of burning, itching welts from those pesky bastards.

Along with building up our muscles and endurance, we had to learn the manual of arms, nomenclature, and disassembly of weapons. There was more drilling, KP, lectures on squad movements, sex lectures, orientation movies and then more KP. The physical training never ended. I can still remember how filthy we got crawling around in the mud and dust during the infiltration course. After that was the close combat course. We went through a mock-up of what must have been a German village with signs written in German.

One of my pals, a guy named Walter Crook, was the second Battalion butcher. Walter was from a very rural part of Georgia and was always spouting off old back country sayings and philosophy. He was a lot older than the rest of us and had a hard time keeping up, especially on the 25-mile hikes. One time we were being taught to drop off a wall, land, roll over and stand right up ready to attack. Well, old Walter wouldn't jump. He argued with the lieutenant for about a half hour and the lieutenant finally told him that if he did not jump, he would climb the wall himself and push Walter off. Walter said he was afraid of getting hurt, but the lieutenant said, "We have good doctors and guys getting hurt is how they get their training. We don't want to deprive them of their training do we?" Walter finally did jump and he didn't get hurt. I don't think the medics were all that disappointed.

The two things I hated the most were the crawling through barbed wire and the gas chamber. We had to crawl under barbed wire fences with a rifle cradled inside our elbows while someone was firing mounted machine guns over our heads. If you raised your butt too high, you would lose part of it. In the gas chamber, we were not allowed to put on the gas mask until after we were inside the chamber filled with tear gas and choking like it would never stop.

The closest town to Camp Claiborne was Alexandria. It was not very big and was surrounded by training camps. There really wasn't all that much to do there. The only way to get to town was to take the bus but the bus didn't come very frequently and this infringed on the time you had on your pass. To make things worse, General Haffner made it very plain that there was to be no hitchhiking.

CHAPTER 3

Alexandria Yom Tov

Major General Charles C. Haffner, Jr. was the commanding general of the 103rd. He was very strong on discipline and military courtesy. One evening, my friend, Corporal Carl Barger from Muskogee, Oklahoma, and I decided we would go to town and as we neared the front gate to wait for a bus, a car pulled up and the man inside asked us if we wanted a ride to town. Barger shouted, "Hell Yes." I climbed in first, sitting next to the driver and I immediately noticed it was General Haffner. Barger liked to talk and even though I kept nudging him, he started to complain about how tough it was to get to town. He hoped that this officer would, if he had any influence with the general, ask him to revoke the damned hitchhiking order. Just then, a car full of officers sped by us. The General made a note of the license plate number on a clipboard that was attached to the dashboard. Barger looked and saw who the driver was and finally shut up, his face very red and very long. When the general dropped us off, I thanked him for the ride and as he said, "You're welcome," he asked us what company we were from. Thank God, he did not ask our names.

When it was time to return to camp, I was on my own as Barger was staying in town that night. It was late on a Saturday night and I was the only one on the bus. I automatically went to the same seat I usually sat on when taking the Dexter bus in Detroit, the closest seat to the rear door. I was anxious to get back to the camp on time and the bus wasn't moving. That is when I got my first introduction to how "colored people" were treated in the South. I yelled up to the driver, "What time does the bus leave?" He answered, "As soon as you get the hell out of the nigger section."

The Jewish High Holy Days were approaching and I asked for and received a pass to go to Alexandria for services. The trip to Alexandria was a pleasure. It wasn't a weekend, and the bus wasn't jammed with GIs. It was heartwarming to find such a warm reception. Alexandria had a very nice synagogue, but not near as large as the ones in Detroit. The services were a little different than what I was accustomed to and I was given to understand that the congregation came from three synagogues that had merged-reformed, conservative, and orthodox. I knew that my parents would be pleased that I attended services. This was one place Kilroy had not been to first.

I was invited to lunch by a couple who were younger than my folks were, but they reminded me of them in many ways. The husband was a local merchant. He was tall and spoke with a soft southern accent. His wife reminded me of a typical southern matron that I might have seen in a movie. She must have been a very pretty woman when she was younger. They told me that they had two married daughters living in other cities. The meal made me feel at home, just as they did. It was typical of the type of meal that my mother made for the holidays, Challah, the Sabbath bread, gefilte fish, chicken soup and roast chicken and potatoes, tea and cookies. It was very difficult for me to believe that people with such deep southern accents were Jewish. It was the most spiritual experience I had while I was in the Army.

Brenner Becomes a Citizen

A few months later, in February, I experienced one of the most important days in my life in Alexandria, when I became a citizen of the United States. I was born in Montreal, Canada and moved to Detroit when I was nine months old. In those days, you didn't automatically become a citizen when your parents did. You had to apply when you turned eighteen.

I applied on my eighteenth birthday, but the papers did not come through until I had been in the service for three months. To say the least, I was proud to receive my citizenship papers at the Federal Courthouse in Alexandria, Louisiana, along with several hundred other men. It was quite an experience meeting men from all over the world who were becoming American citizens while they were already in the American Army.

My adventures in Alexandria weren't always so great. There was usually very little incentive to stay overnight, but one time I did get stuck there when I found I had no way to get back to camp. I couldn't find a place to sleep. No vacancies. I was advised that I might try to find lodging at the dead end of a very quiet side street. When I found the house and inquired of the landlady, she told me I could have a room with another man if I didn't mind sharing. It would be $15.00 in advance, which was a lot of money in those days. She also instructed me not to turn on the light, for the other man was sleeping; just go quietly to the window and my bed would be on the right. I followed her instructions and found the bed. In the middle of the night, I felt drops of water on my face and discovered it was raining and I was under a hole in the roof. At daylight, I awoke and found that I was sharing a room with three other soldiers. When I looked out of the window, I observed that we were in a cemetery in the caretaker's house.

Sometime later, the 103rd broke camp and we went on maneuvers with many other Divisions. As luck would have it, we were still in Louisiana, still in the swamps. It was to be the Red Army against the Blue Army, signified by bands worn on our arms. We had to do everything under wartime conditions. In our case, this meant to get food to the mess kitchens, without getting shot by the enemy. Crook had his butcher block set up under a large tree and was hacking away with a cleaver. Out of the corner of my eye, I saw something moving in the tree behind him-a very long, fat snake was winding itself down the tree. I started to point, speechless with fear, and I never saw that old man move so fast. He hacked that snake into three pieces with that same cleaver. After the initial shock, I started laughing at the look on his face when suddenly I was stung on the tip of my little finger by a yellow jacket, of all things. My finger remained painful and puffed up for three days. So the old saying is true, if the snakes don't get you, the bugs will.

Reader's Digest once had an article about the worst railroad in the world. Naturally, it was in the swamps of Louisiana, where it always broke down. Our job was to get the fresh food up to a distribution point and dole it out from there. We had a couple of sides of beef, and no refrigeration, and wouldn't you know it, the train broke down in the middle of nowhere. We were stuck and the food was spoiling. There were only five of us on that detail with a Lieutenant Perez in charge. He was a tough southern officer but no gentleman. He said, "Fuck it, let's eat." We cut down a pine tree and set the stump on fire. He then cut branches off the tree and shaved the ends off to a point. He cut the meat into huge cubes, stuck them on the sharpened branches and said, "Have at it, each man's on his own," and we commenced chowing down. The lieutenant was quite a guy.

*I remember those heavy barrages.   The enemy artillery
attacks increased and the freezing weather and the
frozen black cold nights made it rougher.
In the early mornings, I often felt that this was the day
I was going to get killed, and sometimes it got so bad, I
wanted to die.
If I'm going to die let it be now, I thought, don't let me
suffer through the next barrage. Let's get it over with.*

CHAPTER 4

Camp Howze, Texas

November 18, 1943

It was just a short time later that we shipped out to Camp Howze, Texas. This was exciting and like a short vacation. We traveled by truck and jeep and I was very fortunate to be in one of the jeeps and here again, we traveled through cities that I had heard of and seen on maps when I was a child. I loved maps in my childhood and made up imaginary trips across the country thinking about people and places I would see. Now there were real people along the streets and they were cheering us on. Camp Howze was different. Instead of swamp it was dusty and barren. We liked it better, for there were more surrounding cities, the closest being Gainesville, and Dallas was the largest. All the people were friendly.

When we arrived at Camp Howze, we realized that we were close to going overseas. We didn't care for some of the sudden changes we were noticing. We started getting replacements of guys from Army Specialized Training Program, (A.S.T.P.) and the Air Corps.

A.S.T.P. was established in December of 1942 by the Army in order to identify, train and educate, academically-talented enlisted men as a specialized corps of Army officers. The A.S.T.P. guys came from major colleges and universities across the country, and were supposed to have received the equivalent of a four-year college education combined with specialized Army technical training over a period of one and a half years. They were used to living in dorms, with maid service and civilian food. They were removed from the program because the infantry desperately needed people right away.

Obviously, it was a shock to suddenly be taken from such places and be put into an infantry unit that was long on physical fitness. It was also rough on the guys from the Air Corps, but for a different reason; they didn't have the physical conditioning we had. Not only that, we were afraid that their lack of infantry training and experience might prove dangerous to them and everyone else when we finally got into combat. Also, the Air Corps, was pretty glamorous. There was nothing glamorous about us.

Every one of these guys was pissed off at the fact that their bright future was cut short by the insatiable needs of the infantry for manpower. The simple fact of the matter is that you had to have someone on the ground, taking it the hard way, to really win a war. You had to have a man with a gun out in front, standing face-to-face with the enemy, in battle. He was the man of the hour. There was no victory without his sacrifice.

June 2, 1944

Reveille. This is getting old. We've been here since November. Up before dawn, run, walk, work and run again. I have never been this strong or fit in my whole life. We line up in front of the barracks and Smitty, a sergeant from E Company, comes up and hands the new 1st sergeant some envelopes.

The sergeant looked at the envelopes and starts reading names out in a loud Brooklyn accent, "Brenner, Chrzanowski, Gulledge, Martin, Petraitis, Sedberry, White! Take these and report to 2nd Battalion, Division Medical Detachment, 410 Infantry."

What now? I suppose they want us to do some sort of shit detail. "Sarge, do you think we will be back by lunch?" Asked Martin. He was always thinking about food.

"You're not coming back, dummy. Don't you know what those envelopes are? They're transfer orders; this here Army is going to make you doctors. Get your gear and get your ass over there."

I couldn't figure out what was going on. I'm no doctor. I thought I might get transferred into special services because of my acting experience. It took a good 30 minutes to lug our gear over to the medical detachment and get our barracks assigned. It was odd, we all took the same place in the barracks that we'd had before. I was glad the guys were all together; all except Chris. The tarpaper barracks were the same, just on the other side of the parade ground.

They didn't teach us very much. We learned basic first aid. We learned how to apply dressings and how to carry guys who were hit. I was pissed off when I heard that medics didn't carry weapons. I had just qualified as expert marksman.

We were issued two medical bags that hung from each side of our rifle belts. There was a lot of stuff we had to carry in them. They were stuffed with sulfa, morphine, bandages and pressure dressings. We had Red Cross arm bands and when we got overseas, we would get white helmets with a large Red Cross on it.

Above:
Combat Medics at aid station meeting. Sy is second left, top row.

According to the Geneva. Convention, or so we were told, the Red Cross symbol was supposed to protect us on the battlefield. The first aid classes were not very informative; I worried a lot about that. Guys would depend on me to save their lives, and hell, I didn't even know if I would have the guts to hold my ground once someone was shooting at me. What if I took off, there wouldn't be anyone to help them. Would I freeze when it came time to act? I was told that my job would be to stick with my squad, no matter where we went, give first aid when needed, tag the injured men with information for the medics at the aid station. I was also to help carry the litters out of harm's way, tag our dead men. We would have to take care of enemy wounded too, if we saw any. Until they told us that, I had never even thought about it.

I took the classes very seriously and tried to learn everything I could. Still, the training was the bare minimum. A Girl Scout would know more than me. This lack of confidence would come back to haunt me more and more as the demands on my abilities would increase later on.

Medic training wasn't always bad, though. We had our little pranks as medics, too. One poor guy was about to get married and we grabbed him in the shower and painted his private parts with the antiseptic gentian violet, deep purple in color, which wouldn't wash off for weeks. He never did tell us what his bride said.

FRIDAY, AUGUST 11, 1944.

THE PERFECT SOLDIER—That was Pvt. Sam Brenner, right, who appeared in full field equipment, plus, on the Camp Howze radio program Wednesday night in a skit prepared by his fellow actor, Pvt. William Barker. Barker also read his monologue, "Wanted: A Song for the Infantry," to soft music by the 410th band.—(Signal Corps Photo.)

Soon after we arrived at Camp Howze, a call came out from special services. Hey, maybe there was still a chance. But no, they wanted volunteers. They wanted to have all the men who were musicians, actors, writers, or had anything to do with show business before the war, report to them. I had done some radio acting before the war but not one person, including myself, showed up. The reason was that we had very little spare time after our regular duties and we didn't want anything to tie up our evenings as well. They started looking through our service records and came up with quite a number of us. We were, "volunteered" to prepare a regular weekly radio show. They came up with a screenwriter,

Left:

Sy cutting up on Camp Howze Radio program

William Barker, who was under contract with RKO Pictures. There were also a number of great big band musicians. The musicians were peeved. They felt they should have been put in special services like most of the big bands were.

Once we got started on the show, everyone pitched in, and I think we even had a little fun, exhausted as we were. The band leader was a high school music teacher. We put on a half hour program, half music and half comedy with me in the lead as Private Joe Pfuf, perfect soldier. Barker wrote a song about the infantry that he sang himself.

As the training intensified, we became more and more aware that we were going overseas soon. Rumors were flying and most of them were true. Best of all, passes were easier to get.

I received my first three-day pass for the long Thanksgiving weekend and with uniform clean and sharp, my expert infantry badge in place, I shared a ride to Dallas. Rooms, as you can well imagine, were impossible to get, but, on this occasion, I found it beneficial being a medic. I was going to the USO to find out where I could get a room. Just as I was walking in the door, I heard someone yell, "Hey, it's the kid from Detroit."

It was Smitty, the sergeant from E company. No dummy, Smitty, like everyone else, wanted to be on the good side of the medics for obvious reasons. "Listen Doc, I have a room at the Baker Hotel and it's yours, all paid for. I found a better looking deal."

There were three really fine hotels in Dallas back in those days; the White Plaza, the Adolphus and the Baker. I'd never been in a place as beautiful as the Baker. Somehow I knew this weekend was going to be special.

The hostess at the USO arranged for me to have Thanksgiving dinner with a family the next day and said there was a dance there that night. I went to the hotel, dropped my things off, and was just going to look around before going back to the USO dance, when a car pulled up beside me. A pretty girl yelled out of the window, "Hi, soldier. Do you want to go to a party? Hop in!"

So, I hopped in, and we drove a little ways, and then turned into a dirt alley. She drove into a garage at the end of the alley. She acted as if this was quite normal, but I couldn't figure out what was happening. We went through her yard and into a door. In the kitchen was an elderly couple she introduced as her parents.

Her father was dressed in overalls but no shirt. He sat at the table drinking coffee and reading the paper. Her mother, who had on a very plain dress and apron, was doing dishes. Neither acted surprised at my presence. I said hello and the old guy just waved a hand, not looking up from his reading.

She ushered me into her bedroom and I was surprised as she started to take off her clothes: good old Southern hospitality! So we had a party. After the party, she said, "That will be ten dollars." I paid her and she dropped me off at the hotel.

Did that just happen? I couldn't believe it. I guess it was just something that was meant to happen. It was what my mother called in Yiddish, ""Beshert"".

I went to my room, cleaned up, put on some fresh clothes and went back to the dance at the USO. I met a very lovely girl and we had a terrific time. I took her out to dinner and a show. I then took her home where I met her parents and then sat on her large screened in porch where we made passionate love for most of the night. I then went to sleep on their glider. In the morning, her mother woke me up and invited me in for breakfast and then she and her dad drove me back to the hotel. We made a date for that night. I took the bus to the home of my Thanksgiving hosts. As I walked from the corner to their home, I had three other invitations for Thanksgiving dinner. People were so very friendly everywhere I went in Dallas. This made quite an impression on me, and I felt great.

Thanksgiving dinner was wonderful. It was a very large, very friendly family. Two of their sons were already in the Pacific. They made me feel so welcome, and wouldn't let me get up without having seconds of everything. It was more Southern hospitality. After dinner, everyone listened to the traditional Texas football game that was as boring as the people were nice. It would have been impolite for me to leave before the end of the game, even though I was anxious to get back to my date. I guess it's like my father used to always tell me, "You never get something for nothing." How right he was, but the price was small. People here were sure nice.

Texas had state liquor stores. You couldn't just go to a bar and order a drink. You had to bring your own bottle and buy setups. I met my date at the USO. It was more convenient, and she brought a bottle of rum. "The war, you know?" She said. We went to the Adolphus Hotel. I ordered cokes, and we had rum and coca cola, just like the song we were dancing to. Our fun was temporarily interrupted, for when we returned to our table, our bottle of rum was gone. Three GI's at the next table raised the bottle in a toast to us and I was about to go over, she grabbed my arm and said, "They aren't worth the trouble." Management must have noticed, as two M.P.'s ushered them out, leaving the empty bottle. We had a very good time in spite of it all and I had another wonderful night on her front porch. The next morning, I was on the bus back to the base. Dallas was a very friendly town and the kid from Detroit had a very sexual three-day pass.

I was with one of the first units to leave Camp Howze on September 20th, 1944. We still didn't know where we were going, east or west. We sure didn't take a direct route, but soon enough we realized, we were heading to the East Coast. It could only mean Europe.

Above:
Cartoon drawn for Sy at Camp Howze

*Everything ran very smoothly like a fine Swiss watch,
with the sole purpose of getting us ready to deploy for
wherever it is we were going.*

CHAPTER 5

Camp Shanks, New York

At the end of a journey that seemed like it might go on forever, we found ourselves at Camp Shanks in New York. We had spent the last days at Howze going through inspection after inspection, making sure all our equipment was in perfect condition. As soon as we arrived at Shanks, we were completely re-outfitted with new stuff.

This was typical of the Army.

In the mountains near the Hudson valley, some twenty miles from the docks of New York, Camp Shanks was run like a factory. No one seemed to really know where we were going, but there were rumors galore. It could be Africa, Asia, Europe, or the Moon. The barracks were different from the black tarpaper walls we called home back at Howze or Claiborne. These barracks, while more substantial, never felt like home; we just weren't at Shanks long enough. This was just a brief stop on the way to somewhere else.

Things moved quickly here. First on the list was overseas orientation. Everywhere you looked, there were men marching from one building to another. There were lectures on how to act on Army transports, how to climb down into a life raft. They talked to us about what we should do about our insurance and where to send our allotments. We had a scary lecture on how to act if we were taken prisoner and how to resist enemy interrogation.

After all the rigorous training we had to get in condition. They sent us to some dog-and-pony medical evaluation to make sure we were fit for battle. If you were breathing, you passed. They checked our throats, our armpits, our butts and our balls. They ran us through a maze of medics with needles and injections to protect us from every possible disease known to man and a few no one knew about.

The best thing about Shanks was the chow. It was really first class and you could eat as much as you wanted. Little did we know that it would be the last time we would have a decent meal in the Army. I visited the PX often in our short stay there and loaded up on Hershey bars for the unexpected. I was wising up to Army life and its many unexpected twists and turns.

I lucked out with a one-day pass into New York City. Before we were given our passes, we were briefed on military security. "Loose lips sink ships," we were told. We had to remove our cactus patches as the location of our unit was supposed to be a big secret. We sure did keep our mouths shut. No one was to tell anyone what unit we were with or where we were located. The funny thing was, we arrived in town on a bus that had, "Camp Shanks" boldly printed on its side.

The bus dropped us off just a few blocks from Broadway. I was thrilled. Some of the guys were lucky and got into see some of the shows, but I was just as happy sightseeing. Four of us went to a nightclub, but it ended up being a clip joint.

Welcome to the War: October 20, 1944

We are on our way. We boarded the USS General J.R. Brooke for parts unknown.

Like anywhere else the 103rd went, the weather over the Atlantic was lousy. There were some older guys serving on the General J.R. Brooke who had been at sea before. They said they couldn't remember ever having seen rougher weather. The storm just got worse with each passing day. I don't think there was one guy I knew of who wasn't seasick.

"ALL MEDICS REPORT TO THE MEDICAL OFFICER!"

The medical officer on the ship looked even younger than we did. He said the men were all sick; they were not eating and it was important that we get some food into them. I asked the ninety-day wonder if he didn't think medics were human, how he expected us to get around that floating nightmare to pass out apples and crackers to all the men, when we were just as sick as they were. He sheepishly told us we'd just have to do the best we could, and we did.

The nights were very black and you couldn't see a thing. During the day, we sat with our backs up against the bulkhead reading. That was when I first heard who, "Perry Mason" was. We were a long way from his world. Anyway, we would finish a book, and then trade it for another one.

I heard someone say they saw the coast of Africa. When I went up to look, I could see it, and to the left, off in the distance, I could see Gibraltar and I said, "Look, the Prudential Building." We all had a big laugh, but later that black night , we heard a loud explosion, which scattered all of us below deck. We heard an alarm and an announcement, "ALL HANDS ON DECK!" We were ordered up in full battle gear, life jackets on. As we approached our previously appointed stations, I saw huge flames shooting into the night sky and a tremendous amount of billowing black smoke coming from a tanker that was pretty close to where we were.

This was it! We were in a real war. Shrill whistles and horns were blowing and the convoy was scattering. We were constantly changing our course. The next morning there wasn't one ship in sight of the General J.R. Brooke. We had heard that there were German U-Boats in the area, but it was just scuttlebutt, or so I had thought.

I was shivering from the cold and shaking from the fear. Thoughts were running through my head,

"Was this the way I was going to die?"

CHAPTER 6

Marseilles, France

October 20, 1944

Soon enough, after passing the Straights of Gibraltar, we entered the Port of Marseilles. This was the first any of us saw of the war up close. There were hulks of ships sticking up out of the water, scuttled by the French to prevent them falling into German hands. The piers and many of the buildings had been severely damaged. We heard that the fighting to take Marseilles had been pretty fierce.

As we began to disembark, it occurred to me that this was the first time we had ever done anything that we hadn't really been trained to do. We went over the side on rope ladders into landing barges and onto the beach at Marseilles.

We were told to be careful. The Germans had heavily mined the port area, along with the rest of the town. One of our majors had his hand blown off as he opened a booby-trapped door. I didn't see it happen, but I heard the explosion. In a way, that is when the war really started for us.

Although I had been alarmed when I saw that burning tanker at sea earlier in the week, the fear went away. Now I began to feel something that didn't seem as though it was going to leave me anytime soon -- A feeling as though something I swallowed didn't go all the way down. I started to feel fuzzy. I wasn't nauseated, as I had been on the ship. Was I afraid? Hell, yes!

But, I wasn't overcome with fear. Not yet, anyway. It's just that it was a very peculiar sensation. Except for that one explosion, it was pretty quiet here. And we were busy so there wasn't time to worry about it. But, that strange feeling just sat there as if it had been attached to my gut and would take some serious surgery to get rid of it.

As scared as I was, being in Marseilles was thrilling. I was on foreign soil, and it was like the start of a new adventure. We spent several days in Marseilles, getting new jeeps and other equipment before shoving off.

We met some French Moroccan troops. They were all over six feet tall and wore bright orange pantaloons with long Aladdin-like curved knives. I'd never seen anything like those knives, and I asked one of them if I could see his knife. When he withdrew it, he purposely cut his finger. He stared at the blade, nodding, as though he was satisfied that it was sharp enough. Astonished, I asked him why he did that. He said with a serious look and a very deep voice, "We do not draw our knives unless we draw blood." I remember thinking at the time that those bright colored pants would make a great target.

When I got a pass for a few days, I teamed up with a guy named Joe from one of the rifle companies. I liked him because he was shorter than I. I was 5 foot, 6 and a half inches, but he was even shorter. At the time, we were sure we were the shortest guys in the Army. I couldn't pronounce Joe's last name, so I called him Joe Spumoni. Joe was Italian and we thought he might be able to understand some French, but he didn't.

While scrounging around, we got hungry and decided to go into a small restaurant. There were about six tables in the place. Two were available and we took the one near the bar. Our waitress, who turned out to be the owner, looked to be in her 60s. Rather plump with curly salt-and-pepper hair, she smelled like cigarettes and garlic. She walked around the place while carrying on a conversation with the other patrons. Joe told her in Italian that we would like to see a menu.

"Monsieur, either your French is very poor, or you are in the wrong country," she replied. Then she said something to the other customers, pointing at us with amusement.

I then asked her for a menu in English. She burst out with a loud, "Ha!", which was followed by prolonged laughter by everyone in the room, after she translated my request.

"The Boch, my little American friend, he has taken everything with him. There is no food. No food for me and no food for you!"

The Germans had taken everything. She offered to make us some boiled onion soup. We then finally realized that though this had been a restaurant, it was not open to serve food or drink now. She just went there, as did her patrons, as that is what they had always done. They didn't know what else to do. We told her we were sorry and that we didn't know they didn't have any food. I didn't want to take anything from her. I felt pretty badly and just wanted to leave. She insisted we have the onion soup. It was not the French onion soup that we would recognize today. I don't think anyone could have felt any lower than we did. We told her we would be back. We returned with two cartons of cigarettes. Cigarettes, in those days in France, were more valuable than money. You should have seen her face.

The Germans had raped the city in many ways. They took most of the cars and trucks. The French people had to improvise using bicycles and wood-burning cars.

One of the things I could never get used to was their damned lack of modesty. The rest rooms were called, "convenience stations." These outdoor latrines were partially shielded by a screen from the knees to the shoulder, so that you could say hello to anyone passing by while urinating at the same time.

Most people who got around on bikes would ignore military traffic. They were both reckless and rude at the same time.

Kids followed us around hoping for chocolate, and they held up their hands in the Victory sign yelling, "Hi Joe!"

Some of the girls we passed waved at us. They wore the shortest skirts I had ever seen and had the strangest hairdos. They would dye their hair the strangest colors, from lavender to green and wear it very high up in the air.

One night, we went to a bar. There was a sailor there who apparently worked in a circus before the war. He was sticking large needles through his earlobes and cheeks, amusing the waitresses. I had some beer that tasted awful, but the company was good, and I joined in with the others telling jokes and drinking that lousy beer.

There were a lot of sailors in the bar, and Joe and I kidded them about having it so much better than the infantry. We enjoyed the good music and I especially liked the torchy songs the French women were singing. It sounded very sexy. The music was coming from an old victrola that they had hidden from the Germans. They said the Germans would have taken the Victrola along with all the records if they had known that it was there.

Our waitress seemed to be standing next to me most of the time and kept pointing to me saying, "You voo-lay voo zig zig?"

At first I thought she was asking if I wanted to smoke a cigarette, then I thought she was accusing me of being drunk.

I said, "No, I'm not ZIG ZIG."

She kept asking. I kept nodding my head, as if to say, "No, I'm not drunk." Later, I found out she was asking me if I wanted to get laid. Too late!

Everywhere we went, kids were yelling, "Hey Joe," and their fingers went up with the V for VICTORY sign. They were begging for cigarettes and bonbons.

One night, I heard the hobnail boots of two combat soldiers coming down the hall. They took me down to the main floor across a dim hall. They pushed me into a room the size of a closet, and had me take the dog tags off a dead soldier. They slammed the door and left me in the room in which I could only stand or squat. The only way to get fresh air was to suck it from the hole left between the floor and door. I screamed for help in between the constant vomiting due to the stench of the corpse and the vomit. It was three days before I was found and let out of the closet. This is one of the nightmares that haunt me the most.

CHAPTER 7

First Fire

November 1, 1944

We pushed on with three days of K and C rations wrapped in a blanket or raincoat; mine hung over the back of my medical belt. We heard that we were about eighty miles from the front and could see the hulks of strafed German vehicles and equipment along the road. Pat White and I got lucky and rode up in back of a supply truck instead of the train that most of the guys were on. The truck was a lot more comfortable than being stuffed in a railroad boxcar. The truck had to slow down and wait occasionally, as the driver was not sure where we were supposed to meet the train, and we had no desire to get to the front ahead of everyone else.

We were climbing the Vosges Mountains. Had this been another time, I am sure I would have found their deep, rolling greenery spectacular. The driver, who had been a history teacher before the war, told me that the Germans had history on their side. No attacking Army had ever won a war or forced a crossing of the Vosges since the time of Julius Caesar.

"These are the foothills of the Alps," he said. "By the time we get to the top of these mountains, we should be above 4,500 feet altitude." He smiled briefly when he looked at us but then his face seemed very anxious. "It's gonna get colder up there."

We just kept going up, keeping up with the train, and it started to rain. The higher we went, the more wrecked German vehicles and tanks we saw. We hadn't been in battle yet and seeing these hulks, some of them still smoking from battle, seemed to trigger that sick feeling I had that started back in Marseilles.

Along with the rain came the wind and cold. God, it was cold! I was used to cold, at least I thought so, coming from Detroit. This cold was different. This was a cold from the inside out. My pack was next to me, and when I looked down, I saw it covered with frost. In the jeep behind us, I saw four guys hunkered down, trying to drive while holding shelter halves up over them to keep dry. I started to think about being a medic. Their fingers could get frostbite. We didn't learn anything about frostbite. Shit. What the fuck are we supposed to do? We had to stop at the side of the road near some houses and people came out of the houses offering us something to drink that at first I thought was coffee. Completely tasteless, it was probably just hot water. Still, they were trying to be nice. One lady spoke pretty good English. She told us Roosevelt was the new President. I had forgotten that there was an election. Hell, he was the old president too. For us, I think he was the only president.

I do not know how long we had been driving, but we finally got where we were going. At least that's what the driver said when he pulled off the road near some tents. We were outside a town called Docelles on November 9, 1944.

Pat and I found ourselves near some medics from the 3rd Division. They had been in it already. They knew what it would be like. We asked them, but they just made jokes. "You'll see soon enough," said one guy as he picked up his gear and started walking back the way we came.

We found Smitty, one of the squad leaders, and asked what was going on.

"Hey," he yelled, smiling at me, "It's the kid from Detroit!" "And the other kid from Detroit," looking at Pat. "Well boys, the 103rd Division has joined the Seventh Army under General Alexander Patch. We are now to become an operational unit of the Sixth Corps, under Major General J.R. Brooke."

I wondered if this was the same General J.R. Brooke the ship was named after. We were green troops, never before in battle, about to play king of the hill with an Army that conquered most of Europe-doing here? Did anyone really believe we could knock them off that hill?

Near the Taintrux River, France, November 11, 1944

The aid station was off the road inside some trees. We could see the river down off to the left across the road. I had my hands deep in my jacket pocket. They were shaking. I wasn't sure if the shaking was from the cold or the fear. I could tell I wasn't the only one like this. Everyone seemed nervous. Today was the day. Today we will see war. All the months of preparation are done. I was assigned to Smitty's squad. I knew all the guys, trained with them. Now they would depend on me to keep them alive. I wasn't sure I could do this. Smitty came down the hill from where I saw all the squad leaders talking. "Hey, it's the kid from Detroit," he said with a grin. "Good to have you with us, Brenner."

His grin lasted only a second. He looked pensive and didn't stop walking around, checking that everyone was OK, giving everyone a good word. I thought I was lucky to be with Smitty. The next thing I knew, we were moving off through the trees. Not running, but walking quickly.

"Keep spread out you guys," Smitty yelled, as he kept looking back at us. I brought up the rear with Tommy Dorsett. After about fifty minutes, I heard Tommy huffing and puffing. I wondered if he was OK, and then I realized I was huffing and puffing too. Sweat was starting to slide down, burning my eyes. We could hear the war. We had been able to hear it for most of the last six days, but now it was much louder. We moved uphill steadily, staying low, keeping in the tree line. The higher we went, the louder the noise became.

Smitty waved us all to a stop. He walked back, checking on each guy briefly. When he came to me, he said it was time to take a breather.

"Why do the machine guns sound different up here?" I asked.

"Cause those aren't our guns. Leastwise, that's what I'm thinking, but shit, Brenner; this is new to me too. You OK?"

I told him I was. I could see some guys from another company moving up the hill to our right. Suddenly, there was a loud, "WHOOSH" sound, and a flash above their heads, and a lot of smoke. It looked as if the treetops just exploded.

"I heard about that," said Smitty, "Tree bursts. The Krauts figure they can kill and maim large numbers of our guys. They shoot their artillery into large trees just below where the major branches depart the trunk; this causes the tree to explode as if it were a giant grenade made of wood-shrapnel. We're going to have to find better cover."

I watched as about half of the other company got up, ran about twenty feet farther up, and dropped below a large tree that had fallen on its side. I wondered why the rest did not get up. Then it was on us. I could hear fire, and the trees and ground around us seemed to be snapping.

"Hit the ground!" Yelled Smitty. I looked up and saw him scooting back toward a large tree to his right. I looked around and was so glad none of our guys was hurt. I looked over at a squad from the other company. The smoke had settled. I recognized Martin, one of our medics, bending over one of their guys.

"Shit," I said to myself, "We're really doing this."

Then Smitty was up and running. "Let's get out of here," he yelled. Suddenly there were flashes and noise all around us. When we got farther up the hill, the pinging sound of bullets started raining all around us. I couldn't see where it was coming from. How could I know where to hide?

We started running up and to the right where there was a large rock sticking out of the ground. The snow on the ground was turning to slush. When we ran past the point where Martin had been, I noticed blood on the snow. "SHIT, SHIT, SHIT, SHIT!" Was I yelling this?

"Medic, MEEEEDIC!" Someone was yelling. He's yelling at me.

It was Red Zimmerman. He was lying in the snow trying to grab at his ankle. I ran over to him, slipping in the slush and having to grab on to a tree. I bent over to see where he was hit. I tore part of his pant leg. There was a little blood, but mostly a clear-colored liquid dripping from his ankle into the snow.

"Are you hurt anywhere else?" I asked, glancing at his arms, head and body.

He didn't answer but shook his head, "no". I poured some sulfa powder on the wound and wrapped it with a pressure bandage the way I had been taught, and gave him some morphine. Tagging him with a brief description of his injury and what I did for him, I told him to sit still and someone would be by to get him. Sure enough, the litter bearers were behind us. We had to keep moving at any cost. That's what they had told us.

I caught up with the squad just as they were moving up over the top of the hill. At the top, guns were blasting, men were yelling, "I'm hit, I'm hit, medic, medic, I'm hit!"

I can't explain what happened next. I don't remember any of it. I guess I went into some kind of a trance. The next thing I can remember, I was laying in the snow next to a tree, and Smitty was resting on one knee next to me. It was quiet, and the air was full of smoke and had an acrid smell.

Later on, I spoke with Pat, and he said the same thing happened to him. In the middle of the nightmare that was around us, we just did what we had to do. We bandaged endless wounds and carried litter after litter back to the aid station. The hardest part was watching guys we knew get hurt. Watching them die.

As the days continued, medics were in great demand. The fighting was fierce. We kept moving up farther into the mountains and closer and closer to Germany. We fought in the forests, on the roads and in the small towns. And we were winning. We were chasing the great German Army as they retreated back across the French mountains back to the German border. The closer we got to Germany, the stiffer the resistance.

The German artillery was everywhere and seemed to go on and on without stop. It got so loud that it was hard to think. All anyone could do was get down and pray.

One time I found Smitty crouched over a soldier next to a tree. It was a German. Just two feet away was one of our guys. I didn't recognize him, but he was obviously dead. The German looked like he was about sixteen years old. I just touched him to see if he was still alive, and he rolled over and his skull fell open. I stared down at it for a few seconds and then I threw up. I have seen this incident in my dreams at least once or twice a week for the last sixty years.

I could hear men praying out loud. There were machine gun bullets splattering the earth all around me, shells bursting, guys running, guys falling, guys crying. It seemed to me that this was too much to comprehend at once. Every morning I would think, "This is going to be my last day." I had these feelings, especially when we were being shelled a lot.

Once, while machine gun bullets were kicking up the dirt beside me, and I was bandaging a wounded man, I heard one of the guys say, "Boy those medics have a lot of guts." He did not realize that I was as afraid as everyone else was. I was doing my job, as all the medics were doing theirs.

I remember the bodies and the wounded men with limbs dangling and stomachs blown open. In the midst of all the confusion, we did what we had to do, never thinking that we would be able to do what we did: Tending to the wounds and carrying the men back to the rear on litters.

Every so often, the Germans would dig in and try to hold their ground. They seemed to do this especially in a built-up area where they could hide in the ruined buildings. They got very good at hiding snipers in church towers. Our guys had to get close enough to the tower to lob some grenades into the belfry. When we were in the forests, we didn't get much help from the tanks due to the terrain. They did help a lot in the towns. When we were in towns or villages, the tanks would blast holes in walls of buildings and then go crashing through the other side.

Fighting in the towns always resulted in a lot of causalities. At least we didn't have to worry about the tree bursts. Our guys would go building-to-building, tossing hand grenades through windows and doorways, as well as dashing into rooms and buildings. Sometimes we used flamethrowers.

One afternoon, we were moving through a village and the troops were going from house to house. The houses were pretty spread out, like individual farmhouses. There was a buck sergeant I didn't recognize waving at me, yelling, "Doc, Doc, in here." As I entered, he waved to me from a stairway, "Up here, Doc."

It was only a few steps up, and turning to my left, I entered a small child's nursery with fairy tale wallpaper. The walls had been sprayed by machine gun fire. Walking farther into the room, I could see an infant in the crib with three bullet holes in its undershirt. Smitty walked in looking for me, saw the baby and was visibly shaken up. He was a real gung-ho guy and had done a lot of killing since we got to France. This was more than he could take. I just looked at him crying. I was in a fog, a complete fog. My eyes were too full of tears to really see what I was doing.

When I finally got control of myself, I gently wrapped the baby in a blanket and carried it out of the house. I handed the baby to an elderly woman, saying that the baby was, "todt", the German word for dead. I could see she didn't understand but I didn't try to explain further. I'll never forget the look on that old woman's face.

That's when I really lost control. Screaming at the top of my voice, I ran up the road in the direction of the retreating Germans screaming, "You fucking bastards, come back and let's finish it, come on, come back and fight like men!" A few of the men chased after me dragging me back to Smitty.

"Are you nuts? They are waiting for us up there." Smitty looked at me with concern.

I started to cry. This isn't right. Why did they show me that baby? I couldn't do anything. They didn't have to show me the baby. They didn't have to call me into that house to see that baby. I didn't have to see this.

My hands were trembling out of control. I stared at them but couldn't stop them from shaking. It infuriated me. I was the medic and I was expected to take care of the wounded, not dead babies. As we started walking away, I finally gave in to the nausea that had been growing in me since I walked into that kid's room, puking my guts out at the side of the road. I didn't like the fact that being the medic made me so popular-that meant that everyone wanted to show me everything.

Everyone was popular when they would get a package from home. Everyone was my friend especially when I would get a kosher salami or some cookies. It was such a warm rich feeling to get stuff from home, not just food, but because hearing about things at home was wonderful too. It was what kept me going most of the time, just so we knew that life wasn't always so hard and sad. Just thinking about home would make anyone feel better.

Most of the guys smoked cigarettes, and I was glad to get cigarettes, as they were used like money during the war. But I smoked a pipe. My sister, Rae sent me a pound of Mixture #79 tobacco every month-enough to last me a whole month. I had learned to smoke a pipe from my Dad. I asked him if he ever smoked cigarettes, and he told me he did when we lived in Montreal before I was born. He said that one day, he had been walking down the street and it was so cold, the cigarette stuck to his lips, and when he tried to take it out of his mouth, his fingers stuck to the cigarette. After that, he started smoking a pipe. He showed me how to pack it so I could smoke it upside-down, and keep my hands warm as well. At night, the glow from a cigarette could be seen from a long distance. It was an open invitation to be shelled or hit by sniper fire. They couldn't see my pipe when it was upside down.

As I'd sit in my hole at night smoking that upside down pipe, I could see my Dad's face, looking like Popeye with the pipe sticking out of his mouth where he was missing two teeth. The only time he had the pipe out of his mouth was on the Sabbath

*The night we crossed the Muirthe River was a real ditch.
The temperature was freezing and the sky was so very
dark.
You couldn't see your hand in front of your face.
I can remember the screams and shells landing all
around us. I felt helpless.*

CHAPTER 8

Thanksgiving in France

We had a hard time keeping track of each other. The mud was so thick and deep that it was sucking our boots right off our feet. Another GI and I decided we were in a minefield. I suggested that the best thing to do was to lay down back-to-back, right there in the mud, and wait for morning where we might be able to see what we were doing. I figured it was better than stepping in the wrong place. With all the rainwater washing off the soil from the mines, we might be able to see them in the morning. We were exhausted and didn't even bother to dig a slit trench. We sat down on our shelter halves back-to-back and covered ourselves with our blankets and raincoats. In that short period of sleep, I kept accusing him of pulling my blanket off of me. When I opened my eyes at dawn, I felt sick to my stomach. I noticed he had died during the shelling. The man who offered to share his shelter half was dead, and that is exactly how I felt. Why him and not me? That question occurred to me almost daily. Was it "Beshert"? I guess it was.

I heard a lot of men crying while in the Vosges Mountains. Groaning in pain and anguish, many would pray out loud, unashamed, in many languages. I'd hear guys screaming, "Don't cut my leg off." I was in the middle of it. This was a time that was very gratifying for the heroic Chaplains and medics. We were the unarmed men of the front lines. Every morning, I would ask myself, "Is this the day I am going to get it?"

Every evening, before sundown, the Germans would send a small single-seat scout plane over our lines to see where we were so they could shell our positions. We could have easily shot him out of the sky with our rifles, but we had orders not to give away our positions. We called him, "Bed-Check Charley."

When we came ashore in Marseilles, we were mostly a group of eighteen and nineteen-year-old snot-faced boys, about to face the coldest winter in recorded European history and the mighty German Army. Now we were men. If there was any snot on your face, it was most likely frozen, and the mighty Germans were on the retreat.

Part of my job as a medic was to help carry the wounded to the rear on litters. When there was time, I'd try to restore supplies in my medical packs so I'd have what I needed. This didn't always happen, as there was rarely time to get everything on my list. One morning during a lull in the action, I got permission to go back to the aid station and load up on supplies. While hiking back, I noticed a lot of new tanks coming up toward the front, parking where directed by the M.P.'s. I asked one of the M.P.'s which outfit they were with. I grinned when he told me, saying I had a good friend from back home with that outfit. I thanked him when he told me where my friend's company was. He never should have told me anything, as I could have been a German infiltrating our lines. This happened frequently, and they often spoke English as well as any of us. Better than some.

I walked on to the aid station, refilled my bags and got permission to look up my good friend, Norman Kirman.

I found Normie sleeping in a slit trench. I kicked him yelling, "Get up soldier!" The expression on his face was priceless, when he slowly woke up and realized who I was.

Above: Norman Kirman

He rubbed his eyes and scratched his stubble beard and shouted, "Is it you?" We spoke for a little while, catching up on news. Much too soon, I had to leave to get back to my unit up front. I didn't see Normie again until after the war.

I had another adventure once while walking back to the aid station. I hitched a ride on an ambulance that appeared to be going in my direction. I was in the back and couldn't see exactly where we were going when we stopped abruptly. When the driver told the MP who had stopped him where we were heading, the MP laughed at us saying, "I wouldn't be in too big a hurry to get there. We haven't taken that town yet." We all had a good laugh about that.

For the most part though, this was a very difficult time for all of us. We couldn't get any rest, as the fighting was continuous. When there was a break, we couldn't dig slit trenches due to the frozen ground. The tree bursts made sleeping difficult as well. Hollywood war movies were never like this.

Men were wounded and dying all the time. Men were having their arms and legs blown off in the heat of battle. It was my job to help them, but most times I felt so useless. I found one guy whose leg was dangling by a thread of skin. His sergeant helped me get a tourniquet on him. I gave him a shot of morphine. I was worried he would lose his leg or bleed to death. I needed to get him to the aid station quickly, even though moving him would be painful. We picked him up and carried him the long way as best we could. By the time we got him there, I was sweating like a faucet, the moisture freezing on my skin. As uncomfortable as I was, the poor guy's pain must have been excruciating.

He was terrified of loosing his leg. "I don't want to loose my fucking leg," he kept yelling. Chaplain William Kleffman[1] came along, and he told the Chaplain that he didn't want to lose his fucking leg.

"Watch your language, your talking to a Priest!" Warned the Sergeant.

The soldier kept thrashing his arms about. "I don't give a fuck who he is."

The Priest leaned over him and told him he would like to offer a prayer and the wounded man said, "I don't think it will work, I'm Jewish."

"That's alright son, I have a prayer for you too," he answered. As a matter of fact he did.

It seemed as though there was no end to the number of wounded men. Some had several wounds of various ages. Each wound had its own distinct odor.

We lived on K rations, rumors, death and fear. With all that was going on around me, all the wounded and dying men, every hour of every day, I couldn't understand why I hadn't been injured or killed. I wasn't any different than they were. They all had mothers and fathers, sisters and brothers. I couldn't understand why I hadn't been hit yet. I guess it was "Beshert". At times, I wanted them to just kill me and get it over with.

The Germans weren't the only reason for the high casualties. Many of the casualties were a result of the weather. The men were complaining of frozen feet and general frostbite of fingers and noses. The more I walked, the more I felt like an icicle. I knew that as the medic, I needed to help the guys get through this.

I told them, "The freezing weather dulls the pain so you guys won't feel it so much." Or I'd say that, "Kilroy arranged the cold weather so he could get there before us."

As the 103rd Division hurled its full weight against the enemy, we took many prisoners. I was surprised to learn that some of the enemy soldiers I took care of were not German. There were many Dutch, Russian, and Polish men, who had been captured by the Germans and forced to serve in the Kraut Army. These forced soldiers told us how they had to kill their German officers in order to surrender.

Thanksgiving was coming up, and we were promised a Thanksgiving meal; a hot Thanksgiving meal. We hadn't had a hot meal since going into action. It was supposed to be a hot turkey dinner for Thanksgiving.

---

1 After the war, The Reverend William C. Kleffman, who had been the Battalion's Catholic Chaplin, was murdered in his Parish House in Omaha, Nebraska on August 27th, 1997. He was about to retire and was planning a trip. His parishioners said he didn't have an enemy in the world. The murder was never solved. Epilogue

That day we were sent out to locate some enemy tanks, and we were bitching because we would miss our Thanksgiving Dinner, but they promised us that they would save us some sandwiches. Our patrol ran across a farmhouse. Smitty sent the point man to crawl ahead and check it out. After listening under a window for a few minutes, he waved us to come up quietly. Using hand signals, he let us know there were three Krauts in the farmhouse making dinner. We could hear them talking and laughing through the window. We waited until they were done and putting their plates on the table. We burst in, taking them prisoner and watched them glare at us as we ate their chicken and potato dinner. It was excellent.

When we got back, we found out that most of the guys who ate the hot turkey we had missed developed a severe case of diarrhea. The epidemic didn't reach its peak until late November. We were the lucky ones after all.

For us, Thanksgiving was hard for more reasons than a bad case of the runs. We knew that our families back home were also celebrating the holiday, and the picture in each man's mind was so clear, of family around the table, together, warm both in body and spirit. I couldn't help but think of my family, all sitting together, snug and warm and safe. I wanted to be with them so very, very much. The feeling that I would probably never see them again left such a horrible sadness inside me. I felt so low that Thanksgiving.

The ever-efficient German Army knew it was a hard time for the American soldier. They wouldn't let this opportunity slip by without taking advantage of it. They started dropping leaflets advising us to surrender. They also introduced us to, "Axis Sally."

Axis Sally

Axis Sally played songs that really made the men homesick. Even though we understood about propaganda, and understood that their goal was to make us homesick, it did have a significant effect on the men; especially married men and ones with special girl friends. Perhaps I was lucky that I didn't have a girlfriend back home in Detroit. Even so, Axis Sally and the music she played still had an effect on me.

HELLO, BOYS! THIS IS SALLY AGAIN... TONIGHT WE WANT TO WELCOME THE 103d DIVISION TO FRANCE. WE WILL RECEIVE YOU WARMLY— VERY WARMLY!

*When we arrived in the French town of
St. Die, we were treated to the biggest battle action I
had yet witnessed.
The Germans were bombing, shelling and machine-
gunning the entire town. But, even as the devastation
progressed, citizens of the town kept emerging from their
cellars, trying to feed us wine and apples. We told them
repeatedly to get back under cover or they'd be killed.
But, they kept coming anyway, often getting in our way.
I have thought of the good people of St. Die often since
then, and I always wondered what it would be like to
go back there some time.*

CHAPTER 9

The Night I Got Killed On the Outskirts of Nothalden, France

November 29, 1944

MY DEAREAST GIRL

Right now while I'm looking at you, I'm looking at your boy.

All I can say is that he's still alive. But the war is a gamble— what's going to happen to him to-morrow, nobody can tell.

However, one thing is certain: Should have the luck of being taken prisoner would be saved.

. While there's life — there's h still has that chance and I take it.—

I know, he'll be wise— —and he loves you.

**So don't worry -
GOOD NIGHT.**

Sometimes when there was a lull in the action, we would sit around the aid station and shoot the bull. We could sit for hours talking and telling jokes. We'd talk about wives and girlfriends, restaurants, and places in our hometowns. We'd talk about what we want to do when the war was over. At the time, we had no idea in the world how difficult it would be to go back to what we understood as normal peacetime life. We simply couldn't imagine how our wartime experiences would change our lives and often haunt us forever after. I know I wasn't the only one who would wonder as each guy talked, if he would ever get back home alive. The jokes were usually about the Army. Often we'd joke about the high command and how they had it so easy. We'd all chuckle at the absurdity of our current situation. I guess the humor was our way of preparing us for what was to come.

On this day, we didn't have much time to talk. We seemed to know that today would be rougher than ever. The official log summary of the day's activities would read (in part) something like this: "The enemy made a counter attack from the direction of Nothalden, using infantry, artillery, and tanks. The 2nd Battalion was pulled back to assist the 1st Battalion on a hill...." But, the official log summary of the day's activities could never reflect how bad things were on that day for the men of the 103rd.

The 103rd received almost non-stop artillery shelling from the Germans. Shells whistled over and through the woods where we had taken cover. My muscles tensed, ready for more, "tree bursts" and wood shrapnel. Our company suffered heavy casualties, including all the officers. Frequently, a guy didn't know he was hit until someone else noticed it.

A buddy would see you and start to yell, "You're bleeding, and you're hit in the arm. Get a medic. Hey doc! Get up here quick."

As soon as I heard the word, "doc" or "medic," I tensed because I knew it meant more blood, more pain, more death; it might even be time for me to die. According to the Geneva. Convention, medics were supposed be off-limits, but that had never stopped the Nazis before. In fact, they went out of their way to shoot and wound medics because they thought it would demoralize the Americans.

I was crouched down in a shell hole, wrapping a dressing on some guy's head when another soldier scooted into the hole. "Hey Doc," he yelled above the noise of battle, "Pat White told me to tell you that Sergeant Neimeyer's jeep hit a mine. He wanted me to make sure and tell you he was K.I.A." I just looked quickly at him, and then back at what I was doing, tears rolling down my cheek onto the dressing. I kept wiping them away with my sleeve so I could see, but they just kept coming. I wanted to scream, but in all the noise, no one would hear.

Neimeyer was my Sergeant in Basic Training. He taught me how to stay alive. Now he was dead. I felt like someone in my own family had died. Guys were getting killed all the time around me, but this was very personal to me.

I got up because I had to get up. I kept going because I had to keep going. It's what Neimeyer would have told me to do. [1] As I trailed the squad up the hill, Corporal Stagg kept motioning me to slow down, not to move up too fast. We came upon a group of GIs who called for me.

"Here's a guy who got hit, Doc, you better take a look."

---

1   In June of 1995, Sy Brenner returned to Europe and found the grave of Sgt. Alfred Neimeyer in the American Cemetery at Epinal, France. Epilogue - Met Roland Prieur- American Embassy cemetery of Monuments

As I rolled him over, his helmet fell off and I saw his face. It was William Barker, that nice guy who wrote the radio program we put on at Camp Howze. I had to tag him K.I.A.. I sat down, cross-legged next to Ray's body and cried.

Everyone I knew was getting killed. I knew I was going to get killed, too. I just wanted it to happen so I wouldn't have to see anymore. I sat there crying for a long time. Someone finally picked me up and shoved me along. The whole day of the 29th continued to be like this. I kept running across more and more wounded and crying men, more and more dead men.

There was a big guy with a large wound to his left hip. I helped him lay down, gave him some morphine, put sulfa on the wound, and wrapped it up with some pressure to stop the bleeding. It was starting to sleet pretty hard, so I covered him with my raincoat. I asked him to let the guys know that the raincoat was Brenner's, and asked that they send it back up to me. After the litter bearers took him back down the hill, I remembered that I had the letter that I wrote to my folks the day before in the pocket. I hadn't had a chance to mail it yet. I wondered if it would ever get mailed now.[2]

That night our outfit took its worst beating. The German heavy counter-attack and Tiger tanks wiped out two American companies. Eighty-six men were killed in action or missing. Seven of them were medics. According to the official record of the action, I was one of the medics who died.

There was so much noise and confusion, I ended up with another company and really didn't know any of the guys. In a way I was glad I didn't know most of the guys. It wasn't good to have friends with you. It wasn't good to see your friends die.

We were sent out to locate the nearest source of German artillery. After dark, a heavy snow covered the ground, and a full moon lit the heavily treed countryside. It didn't take long for us to get lost.

"The god damn snow's covered up all the landmarks," complained the Sergeant.

---

2   In 1948, Sy Brenner was dancing with his fiancé Resa, in the Bowery Night Club in Detroit, when a heavy hand on his shoulder spun him around and it's owner said, "Jesus Christ, I thought you were dead." The hand belonged to that same guy with the wounded hip. He told Sy that when he told the guys at the aid station to return the raincoat to Brenner, they told him not to worry about it, Brenner was K.I.A.. He said the letter did get sent. Epilogue

IPS

WAR DEPARTMENT

THE ADJUTANT GENERAL'S OFFICE

WASHINGTON 25, D. C.

IN REPLY REFER TO:

AG 201 Brenner, Samuel S.
PC-N ET0279

31 December 1944

Mrs. Rebecca Brenner
2537 Elmhurst Street
Detroit 6, Michigan

Dear Mrs. Brenner:

This letter is to confirm my recent telegram in which you were regretfully informed that your son, Private Samuel S. Brenner, 36,547,351, Medical Department, has been reported missing in action in France since 30 November 1944.

I know that added distress is caused by failure to receive more information or details. Therefore, I wish to assure you that at any time additional information is received it will be transmitted to you without delay, and, if in the meantime no additional information is received, I will again communicate with you at the expiration of three months.

The term "missing in action" is used only to indicate that the whereabouts or status of an individual is not immediately known. It is not intended to convey the impression that the case is closed. I wish to emphasize that every effort is exerted continuously to clear up the status of our personnel. Under war conditions this is a difficult task as you must readily realize. Experience has shown that many persons reported missing in action are subsequently reported as prisoners of war, but as this information is furnished by countries with which we are at war, the War Department is helpless to expedite such reports.

The personal effects of an individual missing overseas are held by his unit for a period of time and are then sent to the Effects Quartermaster, Kansas City, Missouri, for disposition as designated by the soldier.

Permit me to extend to you my heartfelt sympathy during this period of uncertainty.

Sincerely yours,

J. A. ULIO
Major General
The Adjutant General

1 Inclosure
Bulletin of Information

Regarding M.I.A. Letter on Previous Page

*Readers Note: On the day Sy Brenner was wounded and taken prisoner, his mother suffered a heart attack as described above. For months afterwards, her family kept the news of him from her, intercepting mail addressed to her telling her that he was missing in action. The Army reported him as MIA because they did not find his body but they believed him to be dead as several soldiers who returned to the American lines reported seeing him die in the explosion. Sy's sister Rae would read old letters from Sy or make up new ones to keep her mother from thinking that there was something wrong. Here is a copy of a letter sent to Mrs. Brenner.

The Red Cross arranged for Sy's brother Myer to get a furlough to come home due to Sy's status. He had enlisted the day after Pearl Harbor and was in Pearl Harbor one week later where his expertise as an engineer was sorely needed. Myer hadn't been home since. When he left to go back to Hawaii, he handed an envelope to Rae saying, "Give this to the kid when he comes back."

When she looked at him questioningly, he said, "The kid will come back!" Inside the envelope were five one hundred Dollar bills and a letter telling Sy that he wasn't allowed to use the money for anything other than to have a good time. It also said not to worry where the money came from because he won it in a crap game. That was very typical of Myer.

This guy was no Smitty. He didn't seem real sure of himself, but he also didn't seem to want to ask or take advice from the more experienced guys. It soon became obvious that we were on the wrong side of the enemy lines. Nevertheless, we had a job to do.

We worked our way through the snow and woods toward the place we thought the artillery fire was coming from. Using the flashes from their firing blasts as a beacon, we spotted six Tiger tanks below in a small valley; they were lined up about a hundred yards to the right of a barn. There was a farmhouse to the left of the barn. We immediately got on the radio with the coordinates of the Kraut tanks. The second we finished transmitting the location, the tanks started to move, guns pointed at the treetops just above us.

It was a very light night, and there was a lot of snow on the ground. Another man and I ran toward the shadow of the farmhouse, figuring that if we got into the shadow of the farmhouse, they might not see us. While running, I glanced back over my shoulder and saw the 88 on the tank swivel, and all I remember was seeing a blinding flash.

Right after the flash, I said to myself, "I love you Ma and Pa. Shema Yisrael, Adonai elohenu, Adonai echod."[3]

---

3   Shema Yisrael is the fundamental Jewish affirmation of faith: "Hear O Israel, the Lord our God, the Lord is one."

Detroit, Michigan, November 29, 1944

A full moon lit the early evening sky, jumping in and out of the clouds. Below, on the city streets, the wind dragged recently fallen snow from one drift to another. Like so many others this winter, an icy storm had blown in from Canada. Despite the tempest, things were quiet inside the modest home at 2537 Elmhurst Street where Rebecca and Morris Brenner lived. Two gold stars hung in the front window, a sign anyone at the time would have known meant this family had two sons in the service. Their widowed daughter, Rae had just finished tucking her two daughters into their upstairs beds. Morris was listening to the radio in the living room and reading the Daily Forward, a Jewish newspaper. Rebecca was in the kitchen doing the dishes.

Rae bounced down the stairs humming and headed for the kitchen to help finish the dishes. As she got to the kitchen door, she heard a heavy thud. Bursting into the kitchen, she saw her mother lying on the floor, clutching her chest. "Ma what's the matter?"

Rebecca grimaced, "My son. My baby," she whispered.

"Ma, what do you mean?" Rae knelt down beside her. "Where is the pain?"

Tears streamed down Rebecca's face, and she began to sob. "My son, my baby, my poor Seymour! He's been hurt!"

"Pa, Pa! Call an ambulance and come here quick. Something's happened to Ma."

Nothalden, France, Shortly after midnight, November 30, 1944

As I regained consciousness in the snow, a German soldier was kicking me in the ribs and screaming, "Raus! Raus!" A second soldier held an American .45 two inches from my nose and a third soldier stood at my feet holding a hand grenade, poised like he was going to throw it at me. Unbeknownst to me at the time, one of my companions had managed to escape; when he'd gotten back to our lines, he'd reported me dead.

I wasn't scared. I guess that I was in shock since I should have been scared. All I could think of was that if he threw that grenade, he would kill us all. The farmhouse was still burning and lighting the darkness. I could feel its warmth in spite of the cold. I could feel the blood coagulating on my nose and pain wracked my body. I realized I had been wounded in the hands, left hip and face. My helmet was gone.

As I lay there, dazed in the snow, I realized that the soldier I had been running with was lying there too. To my surprise, he told me that he had broken my dog tags in half so that the Krauts wouldn't know that I was Jewish. I didn't know how he knew I was Jewish. I didn't even know his name. He said he had told the Germans that I had the wrong blood type on my old tags and was supposed to be getting a new set of tags. Who was this righteous Christian, gone so far out of his way to save my life? Maybe he was Jewish himself. I never found any trace of him in the records of the Division or the battle, nor did I encounter a mention of him in the P.O.W. Bulletin. From that moment forward I couldn't even remember what he looked like. No matter; it was "Beshert", meant to be.

"Raus! Raus! Mach Shtill!" Bellowed the German, with his pistol still pointing at my head.

My companion helped me up, and we were herded over in front of the barn. A fourth German set a machine gun and pointed it directly at us. We both felt certain we were about to be executed.

In our many battles through the Vosges Mountains, it was not unusual to find murdered American soldiers with their own weapons stuck in their mouths. The Germans were angry and confused. Hitler and his generals bragged that the Americans would never fight their way through these mountains; they were too soft. For a change, I felt fortunate as a medic that I could not carry a weapon of any kind.

American artillery fire continued pouring like rain on the Germans, exploding all around them and shaking the earth. It was freezing cold, and I realized my body might be going into shock. I began to shiver; the only source of warmth in the burning farmhouse. I was worried we might get killed from friendly fire before the Germans could kill us. My companion tried to whisper to me, but the noise was deafening.

This guy almost certainly saved my life. I tried to ask him his name, but every time we tried to talk to each other, the guy with the machine gun would yell, "Mach shtill," warning us to be quiet.

With my body and hands throbbing, I rubbed myself in silence. The Germans didn't seem to mind the shell fire and were staying put. We could hear them rattling their mess kits and talking very loud, which is something that we would never have done. Some of them sounded like they were drunk, one laughing loudly and waving a bottle of Schnapps.

I was lucky that I wasn't hit too badly. I had shrapnel all over my face, most of it from my helmet and all over my hands. For many years after the war, I would chew on the side of my cheek, biting out small pencil-point sized pieces of shrapnel. My medical kit and web belt had a big hunk torn from them, which probably saved my life, as the flying metal didn't go all the way through.

My hands were freezing, and I tried to keep them warm by shoving them deep into my pants pocket. That's when I realized that when they searched me, the Germans overlooked the small penknife my father had given me just before basic training. When he had given it to me, I had laughed, saying that the Army would give me a nice big one. He said to keep it anyway, adding that you never know when it will come in handy. Acting like I was wiping blood from my hands onto my sleeves and without the Germans noticing, I was able to cut the inseam of my pants behind the belt buckle and slide the small knife in there.

Unfortunately, they did find my pipe and tobacco. One of the guards took my pipe, putting it in his mouth, filled with my tobacco saying, "Ya, Americanisher Tobac. Gut, ya gut."

Seeing him smoking my pipe was the start of the terrible humiliation that we as prisoners faced every day.

As the first hint of daylight began to find its way between the trees and through the smoke, we were moved into a desolate, shell-damaged barn. A German officer materialized and paced up and down in front of us with his hands clasped behind his back, his shiny boots were able to avoid the filthy, slushy rubble on the ground. He looked like he just walked out of the wardrobe department of a movie set. Tall and statuesque, his uniform was spotless. His boots were shiny and un-scuffed. He turned his steely gaze to the quivering mass of huddled GIs in front of him and intoned in flawless English, "For you, the war is over. If you try to escape, you will be shot on the spot."

How could he keep those boots so clean in this kind of weather?

He had us split up into two groups. The guy who probably saved my life that freezing November night was marched off with the other group, and I never saw him again. I never did find out his name.

His group was herded into some boxcars. The boxcars were so crowded that the men had to remain standing the entire time. They received no food or water. The sanitary conditions were so bad, they had to relieve themselves right where they stood.

Apparently, the Krauts felt we were in better condition since they forced us to walk.

It took three days to get us over the Rhine River.
For, every time they built a pontoon bridge, our P-47s
would bomb them.
Once we finally crossed the Rhine, we all walked up to
trees to urinate and said to each other,
"I always wanted to piss on Germany."

CHAPTER 10

The Death March: My walk into hell

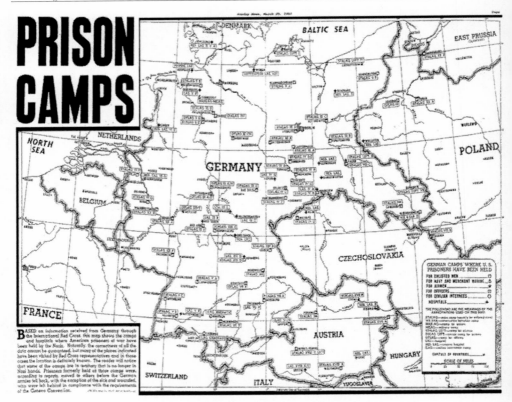

PRISON CAMPS

Above: Prison Camps in Germany

As we marched into Germany, they kept reminding us that if we tried to escape or fall behind, we would be shot. They not only meant it, but they did it. I'm still haunted by the vision of that march: Two seemingly endless columns slowly snaking up the road, three prisoners abreast, a yard or so between the columns.

Most of the men were badly wounded, and they wouldn't let us take care of them. It got colder as we went on. It didn't take us long to realize that we were not going to be fed or receive any water. We tried to help each other, but things got so bad, we had trouble taking care of ourselves. The guards would prod us along with their rifle butts, hitting our backs and necks and shouting, "Mach Schnell!"

They just loved to use those rifle butts. I started to play a little game with myself, betting on which side would get hit next. I guess it helped keep my mind off of the horrible situation. We walked the whole way in fear. Every so often we heard the crack of a rifle shot from somewhere behind us. I was sure that meant another one of our guys ended up dead on the road. It was miserable, piercing cold! I felt like a walking icicle, and my runny nose was freezing on my upper lip. I was afraid my nose would fall off.

The Germans, with their heavy overcoats and scarves, were keeping warm by swinging their rifles around at us. In their eternal wisdom, the top brass who planned our operation, like himself, we were told, hadn't bothered to supply us with warm winter clothing; they expected the war to end soon. They even had the nerve to tell us that we'd be home by Christmas! So here we were in the midst of the coldest European winter on record, and all we had on were light field jackets, light woolen caps and gloves. In fact, it was so cold, that when we had to relieve ourselves, our fingers were too numb for us to unbutton the fly on our trousers. So we had to urinate in our pants, which warmed us up at least for a few minutes.

Time didn't seem to have any meaning. Days turned into black, frozen nights and back into day, and we just kept walking. The monotonous routine seemed to be our whole life. We would get a brief break every two hours when the guards were changed. We were not allowed to have any fire to warm us on the breaks. When we asked for food or water, they just laughed at us. Being a medic, I felt that I should be helping the other guys, but I was helpless as the Germans had taken away my medical bags when they captured me.

When I asked for bandages for the men, they just replied, "Nicht vershtehen (I don't understand)." I knew some of them spoke English because sometimes they would give us orders in English.

The wretched conditions didn't keep us from trying to screw up the Krauts' system every chance we got. We hit them with our favorite prank whenever they halted the march to change the guards, about every two hours or so. As we rested, the guards would count us; while the tally was in process, three or so guys from the front of the column who had already been counted would scoot to the back, throwing off the count. On many occasions, we were able to pull this off three or four times at each halt. This gave us more time to rest since they now had to start counting all over again, really pissing off the Krauts. How we managed to keep straight faces as we did this, I'll never know.

During the nights, I was thinking about my parents, wondering how they were and knowing that they were worrying about me. I had no real idea where I was or how long we'd been marching through the constant snow and howling winds. I knew we had crossed the Rhine, but that seemed almost from another lifetime. My back ached from the incessant blows of the German rifle butts. Pain shot up my legs with each step, and my feet had turned a strange gray. I feared they might be frostbitten, so at each opportunity, I kept rubbing them to aid the circulation.

As we were marching, we came to a small town, and they stopped us in front of a small framed red and white building. It reminded me of a little schoolhouse. This was far from being a schoolhouse. It was Gestapo Headquarters. Each man was taken in individually and interrogated, some brutally. I heard screams but we all, I am proud to say, gave them nothing but our name, rank, and serial number.

I was lucky they did not look at my dog tag and dismissed me only as a, "sanitator" (German for medic). They seemed to know more about us than anyone could imagine. They even knew where we received our training. Strangely enough, the Germans never photographed me or took my fingerprints; not even when we arrived at our final destination.

Our interrogators wore heavy leather black coats and had black felt hats with the brim snapped down. After all we had heard about them, it was a very scary situation. I tried not to show my fear.

After we left that town, they continued to march day and night, farther and farther into Germany. They never offered us anything to eat or drink. One day, as we were marching along, a column of German soldiers were marching in the opposite direction and one stuck out his hand as he was about to pass me. I automatically stuck out my hand too, and he gave me a small, warm red potato. I felt guilty, being the only one having the only morsel of food in days.

It was shortly after that, I got the shock of my life. Added to our column was Chris, the guy who had trouble with my being Jewish back in basic training. My body turned to jelly. How well I remembered his cutting anti-Semitic insults. I was terrified he would give me away to the Germans; a fear that never left me the whole time I was a prisoner. Believe it or not, he never said another thing about it.

Each day, they would add more and more American prisoners. I couldn't tell how many days the march lasted; ten days, twelve days, two weeks. Time seemed to drag on and on with us getting weaker and weaker due to lack of sleep and food. As men would be added, others would be subtracted, dead from their wounds or shot by the guards. This was turning out to be a real death march.

As we marched along, I thought of Colonel Selk back in basic training, yelling, "Only ten more miles men, only ten more miles." Every so often, I would say that to myself and somehow it helped me get through to the end of the march.

As we were nearing the city of Freiburg, they stopped us and separated us into groups of twenty-five. We were then placed in two columns and marched into a railroad yard with many boxcars and freight trains. The opposite column from mine was loaded into the boxcars. Stuffed in like sardines, the men were yelling and couldn't move. The roofs of the boxcars were well ventilated with .50 caliber bullet-holes.

I was lucky that I wasn't in the group that was loaded onto the boxcars. We later learned that our own planes strafed them.

The Allies had heavily bombed Freiburg, and the people there were angry. Most of the city had been completely leveled. When the civilians saw us, they came at us with everything they could get their hands on-hammers, rakes, and shovels. The only thing that saved us was the air-raid siren and the guards telling the crowd that we were, "Nicht fliegers" (not fliers).

Founded in the Twelfth Century by the Dukes of Zahrain, Freiburg, once the most attractive city in southern Germany, was now a city in ruins. Due to the air raid, we marched into the woods and away from the train station. We wouldn't be able to ride the rest of the way by boxcar as the others did. Later, we were back on the road marching. The air raid was a blessing for us because it gave the guards plenty of time to get us away from the angry citizens.

Leaving Freiburg and heading into the Black Forest, we marched for several more days, again without food, with little water and with plenty of whacks on the backs and necks with rifle butts. We didn't know how many days it took, but we finally ended up at Stalag V-A, our home for the next six months.

It's not the very worst of my regularly recurring nightmares, but almost. It visits me at least once per week; even sixty or more years later: I see myself fast asleep, face up, on a cold, hard-packed dirt floor. A sharp pins-and-needles sensation inflames me from the shoulders up, waking me suddenly; a pack of large rats, maybe fifty or sixty in number, scurry all around me, some running right over my face-eyes, ears, nose, mouth and neck.

Not until this point (in real life) do I wake up in terror, feeling as if I'm drowning.

CHAPTER 11

Ludwigsburg (near Stuttgart), Germany

Mid-December 1944

The guards continued to prod us along by hitting us in the back and neck with their rifle butts. We didn't know what time it was, or what day it was, as we staggered along on that freezing death march into the town of Ludwigsburg. I don't know how many men fell out or died along the way. I don't know how many were shot because they couldn't keep up. All I know, is that we arrived with a lot fewer men than we started out with. It wasn't until years later that French Red Cross records confirmed the death march had taken us fourteen foodless, waterless days.

We were led into a large barn-like building constructed of large sheets of tin. There was no heat in the structure and no insulation to shield us from the freezing cold weather. As I shuffled inside, I was hit immediately by a foul stench that instantly nauseated me. This huge building was crowded with men in various uniforms, walking around or lying on the cold dirt floor covered with straw and debris. We felt utterly degraded, stripped of all individuality, dignity, and humanity. My feet were sore beyond belief, and my toes were frozen, a hideous grey in color. Since they had taken our medical pouches, I couldn't even take care of my basic needs.

On the far side of the room was a large group of French naval officers in their white uniforms. Seeing them, I thought of the French fleet, scuttled at the bottom of the harbor in Marseilles.

Surrounded by hundreds of men in the same situation, I felt very much alone. Once the nausea began to settle, I found a spot on the floor and lay down. After so many days of marching along without much food or rest, I was exhausted. At first, despite the dirt floor, I felt very comfortable until I realized that I was now covered with lice, and they were eating me alive. Later, when we complained to the guards, they just laughed at us.

Sanitary conditions were awful. The toilet was a large pit outside covered with lime and slime. The pit was approximately twenty feet long by five feet wide. There was a tin roof and open sides. On the side of the pit was a long telephone pole. You had to sit on that pole and shit over the side. The pole was covered with shit, vomit and urine. The stench coming from the pit was unbelievable. Many of the men had diarrhea, and there was never enough of the strange toilet paper that had wood slivers in it. Next to the pit was a water pipe sticking straight up three feet out of the ground. By opening the spigot, you could get water to wash with or get a drink. The water was freezing cold. Joe Parys, a guy I knew from the 45th Division, told me that his buddies suspected another prisoner of stealing a piece of bread, so they had picked him up and thrown him in the slime pit. They never saw him again, but later they heard the guards fished him out.

That night, I fell into a deep sleep, exhausted from the long march. I was terrified to wake up finding large rats crawling over my body and across my face. I was too scared of the rats to go back to sleep as I slapped at them, trying to keep them from me.

In the morning we were given a cup of ersatz coffee that tasted terrible, but was most welcome. The other prisoners resembled animals when it arrived, swarming and pushing and shoving, a crazed stare filling their eyes. In their panic to possess something warm, they almost knocked over the buckets of coffee.

Later in the day, several guards came in led by a Feldwebel, which I later learned was a sergeant. They selected several men, myself included, and marched us out of the barn, away from the camp toward the train tracks. One of the guards, in quite good English told us that we were going out on a work detail to clean rubble away from the train tracks. The freezing temperature made it miserable trying to work with our bare hands. The guards watched, wearing long, very warm looking overcoats, their hands in the pockets to protect them from the weather. We had nothing but a light field jacket. Without gloves, my frozen hands ached, as I had to pick up parts of tracks, bricks and debris. The guards yelled, "Mach schnell!" and "Mach shtill!" at us all the time, and continued hitting us with their rifle butts, pushing us to work faster.

We were all dragging from exhaustion when we finally returned to that lice-infested barn. As bad as the place was, I was looking forward to lying back down on that foul smelling floor. I was really that tired; I didn't care what I might be lying in.

As soon as we walked into the door, a very young kid with a red beret and an English accent called out, "Sick call, over here." One of the other prisoners said, "I know he doesn't look old enough, but that English paratrooper is really a doctor. You better go over and have your face looked at. If you are lucky, you'll get taken over to the Lazarett across the street."

"What's a Lazarett?" I asked.

"It's an old World War I cavalry stable across the road from the gate. I think it means hospital, clinic or something like that; but, it's run by the prisoners, not the Krauts. During World War I, the Kraut cavalry kept their horses downstairs and the men slept upstairs. Anyway, it's a lot cleaner and nicer than this shit hole we're in now. I got to go over there when I first got here and actually had a bed to sleep in for two days till they kicked me out 'cause I wasn't sick enough."

I looked out across the road and saw an old brick building surrounded by barbed wire with a gate facing the gate to the compound we were in. There were machine gun guard towers at each corner of the fenced-in area.

An English medic who worked with the doctor lined us up, and they did what they could for us. Without supplies, there wasn't much they could do. A lot of the guys were pretty sick with pneumonia, and they were taken out of the barn.

Just before dark, we were brought our second, and last, helping of coffee for the day. I ran and pushed and shoved to get my share. I felt no humility. I felt no shame. Stripped of all dignity, I swore to myself that in the future, I would steal or even kill before I would ever go hungry again. I had become an animal.

They say that memories are made so that we can smell the roses in December. My memories were wilted in the spring of my life.[1]

---

1   When taken prisoner, Sy Brenner weighed 160 pounds. When he was liberated, he weighed 97 pounds and lost all his hair.

Each man had a distinct odor of his own from various wounds. Some of your buddies got killed, but you try to bear it. You keep the tears to yourself and try not to show it. You're as brave as the next guy.

CHAPTER 12

The Lazarett

The next day, while the Germans were photographing and fingerprinting the new prisoners, a guard walked through the barn seemingly looking for someone. He walked right up to me and pulled me out of the I.D. line. So they never did get my picture or my prints, and they never found out I was Jewish.

"You Sanitator, ja?" The guard asked, pointing at my armband.

"Ja," I answered anxiously. I knew that sanitator meant medic.

"Kommen sie," he said, motioning me to follow him with his hand.

He led me out of the barn into the frozen air. As I followed him out the gate and across the muddy road, I felt a chill in my arms and neck. At the time, I wondered if it was from fear or the weather. We went straight through the gate to the Lazarett (German for sick-bay), a two-story structure. There was a concrete step going up to a small landing at the entrance of the building. Standing on that step was a very spiffy officer in a German colonel's uniform topped with a very warm looking leather coat. The sunlight glistened from the top of his shoes and off the brim of his hat. He had short, gray hair and a small, jagged scar on his chin. Standing there looking down at me, he was very intimidating. Though, in reality, he couldn't have been much taller than my five foot six and a half. He had a stocky build and a thoroughly military bearing. He walked with a slight limp but affected a swagger to show that he was a man of importance.

Next to the Commandant, stood a prisoner wearing a heavy gray overcoat with chevrons on the sleeve. I assumed the guy was a prisoner, but I didn't recognize the uniform. I had never seen one like it before.

The prisoner stepped down toward me as we walked up, and turned toward the officer, but spoke to me, "I'm Henk Das. I'm Dutch. I'm going to be your dolmetcher."

I looked at him puzzled and he explained, "Your interpreter." Nodding his head toward the officer, "This is the Commandant." He was jabbing me in the ribs gently with his elbow so I would understand that I should salute.

As the Commandant began to speak, in German of course, I could actually understand most of what he was saying. I understood Yiddish, but until that minute, I didn't realize how close the two languages were. I made an immediate decision that it would be better not to let anyone know I understood what they were saying. If I accidentally started talking German-sounding Yiddish, but said the wrong word, they would be able to figure out that I was a Jew.

Henk translated that I was to go inside to the guard's bathroom on the first floor, clean myself up, and then go to the prisoner's hospital on the second floor and assume my duties there. I was to be in charge of the Verbandzimmer.

I asked quietly what the Verbandzimmer was. He then told me that the Verbandzimmer was the bandage room. "That's where you will be most of the time," he said, "and that's where you will be doing surgery."

I asked Henk what that all meant. He said that by order of the Commandant, I was now in charge of the bandage room and the surgery.

I started to protest that I was just a first-aid man and not in any way qualified to do surgery, but Henk signaled me to keep quiet. He later told me that the Commandant couldn't care less if I was qualified and it was not healthy to contradict him. "You are anything he says you are. Don't forget that!"

We both saluted again, and the officer walked off back in the direction of the main camp. Henk showed me into the guards' bathroom so I could get cleaned up. Boy, did it feel good to be able to wash with real soap and warm water.

As he started to explain what my duties would be, I realized how lucky I was to have Henk with me. At five foot nine and very thin, he was your typical blond Dutchman, except that he never spoke with an accent. He told me he spoke seven different languages. He explained that there were prisoners at the camp from all over, and he was able to speak to almost all of them.

After I finished washing up, I followed Henk up a wide concrete stairway to the second floor. At the top of the stairs was a long hallway to the left. To the right was the entrance to a bathroom facility that in the Army was called the latrine. The latrine had a couple of urinals and one toilet and two sinks. We entered the first room on the left.

"This is the Verbandzimmer," he explained, "the bandage room. This is where you will work. We had an English doctor here until yesterday, but they sent him away. Now you are here in his place."

What the hell am I doing here? I'm not a doctor. I never even worked in an aid station. What am I going to do if someone is really hurt?

He could see I looked overwhelmed by all that was happening to me. "Don't worry," he said. "You have an assistant who can show you around. His name is Paddy Green. He's a British paratrooper. He was one of the red berets that dropped behind the lines at Arnhem.   I'll go get him; he should be here to show you around."

While waiting, I looked around to see what we had to work with. Along one wall was a long table that had a small sterilizer on it. It also had a set of surgical instruments, a dozen rolls of toilet paper with wood slivers in them, rolls of cotton batting (to use in place of gauze to cover up an open wound), and a liquid called Kalen. I wondered what Kalen was. The cupboard was pretty bare, but there was some good news: running water and a latrine next door, which appeared to have been kept reasonably clean. In the middle of the room was a long wooden table that I assumed was for putting stretchers on.

In a minute, Henk returned with a very short, stocky fellow who had very short red hair. He had on a British Airborne uniform with a red beret and brown boots.

"Paddy, this is Sam Brenner. Sam is going to be in charge of the Verbandzimmer. The Commandant wants you to assist him and tell him what you guys do in here."

Paddy had a blank look on his face and nodded toward me in recognition. Something in that expression told me Paddy and I would never be friends, which was surprising in that I otherwise tended to get along pretty well with Brits in all their flavors - Aussies, Kiwis (New Zealanders), Scotties and Jocks, and Taffies from Wales. I made out OK with the other Paddies from Ireland, and even the colonial troops from India, who had some very strange habits (such as cleaning their anus with their forefinger, then their teeth, first thing each morning). But, my assistant, Paddy Green would always be a tough nut to crack.

Now he explained in a very cold way that the other medics would bring me patients who would need treatment, such as bandaging and to have their wounds cleaned. "Sometimes we have to do surgery as well," he said matter-of-factly.

I looked at him amazed, but guessed that he was pulling my leg. Still, there was that Limey doctor here before. He probably did do some surgery if it was needed.

"I guess we won't have to do that anymore, at least until they get us another doctor."

"Hey Yank, didn't Henk tell you?" Paddy asked with a sneer on his face, "You're in charge of the Verbandzimmer. That means you do what has to be done."

"But I'm not a doctor. I can't do surgery." Surely he could understand that.

"You bloody well are going to do whatever needs to be done."

I decided to change the subject. "Where do we get supplies?" I asked.

He looked at me with a blank face, like he didn't understand what I was asking.

"You know, stuff like sulfa, bandages, gauze and stuff like that. Where do we get it from?" I asked again.

He stared at me blankly again for a few seconds and then turned walking toward the window and started turning his head slowly from side to side in a gesture of disbelief, whispering more to the wall than to me, "You Yanks." Then turning toward me, he looked at me like I was some kind of fool.

In a much louder voice he asked, "Where the bloody hell do you think you are? We don't have things like that," he answered with a sneer.

"What about morphine?" I asked.

"You Yanks." He muttered under his breath, shaking his head from side to side again, turning back toward the window.

The room became very quiet. What had I done to piss him off?

I looked around the room, feeling very uneasy about how he was acting towards me. Hanging from the center of the ceiling by a black electrical cord was one very weak twenty-five watt light bulb. Other than the window, it was the only source of light. Trying to think ahead about what we had to do, I asked Paddy to help me move the table closer to the window where we would have more light to work with. I had seen the docs at the aid station working near a window for extra light.

"You Yanks," he muttered again.

I could see that he wasn't going to like anything I said or did. Well, fuck him. I didn't ask for this. And I didn't ask to be put in the Verbandzimmer either.

Not until much later did it occur to me what Paddy's problem might be: He'd been a P.O.W. and stuck in this lousy camp for a long time now. Before I showed up, he'd been in charge of the Verbandzimmer, and he was probably a lot more knowledgeable and experienced than I'd ever be. Now here was this upstart, "Yank" whose mere presence had pulled the rug right out from under him. No wonder he was so pissed off and nasty.

After shaking his head some more, he did move over to the other end of the table and helped me move it closer to the window. The table was heavier than it looked, and there was obviously a lot more light on it when we got it next to the window. Shaking his head some more, Paddy walked out the door and down the hall.

Henk Das was just outside the door talking with two other guys, both in American uniforms. What shocked me was that one of them looked like a Jap. Considering that I'd never seen a Japanese person before, even in Detroit, imagine my surprise at meeting one here in a German prison camp, dressed like an American soldier.

Henk introduced us. "Sam, this is Masa Uchimara. He takes care of the TB patients." We shook hands. "This is Jacques, one of our Frenchmen." He then explained that we had several French patients at the time. Jacques had a bandage on his forehead, but otherwise looked to be in excellent condition. We shook hands. I said, "It's so cold in here, it's a wonder that we all don't have pneumonia." We all laughed.

I learned from Jacques that Masa had been captured in Italy. He told me that he worked down at the opposite end of the building where all of the patients with pneumonia and TB were. As the soft-spoken Masa said in his own words, these were the, "unwanted prisoners." He had nineteen of them at the moment with pneumonia and six who showed signs of tuberculosis.

I found it hard to assimilate the idea that here was a man who in the eyes of most Americans represented the enemy, but who was a real American hero in every sense of the word.

Masa Uchimara

He had been a medic with the famous 442nd Combat Team when taken prisoner, a unit composed entirely of Japanese-American soldiers. Not until after the war did I learn that this was the most highly decorated of all American combat regiments.

Masa told me his brother was in the same unit; they hadn't seen each other for a long time when suddenly there they were together on the battlefield. To my amazement, he said he had another brother fighting in the Pacific, serving as a translator. I learned that his mother had died when Masa was thirteen years old, and that since the start of the war, his father, was "doing his time" in an internment camp with other Japanese and Japanese Americans. Other than these bits of information, Masa never said much about his family, and he never complained about his own injuries, or how much he suffered from hunger. I knew from the moment we met that we had a lot in common-he was so modest, so low-key and down-to-earth. Throughout the rest of our time together in the camp, Masa seemed comfortable as part of our group. He didn't joke around as much as rest of us, but he always joined in during the bullshit sessions that took place late into the evening before the lights went out, usually listening intently to the conversation, clearly happy to be included.

Masa Uchimara

Before meeting Masa, the tension in the air had been thick enough to cut with a knife. That all evaporated in the in the blink of an eye, though. Next on the agenda of this amazing afternoon, Henk showed me a room directly across the wide hallway from the Verbandzimmer, the room some of the American medics slept in. The space was quite narrow: a lot smaller than the Verbandzimmer, and not having a window. It was a lot darker as well. A crudely constructed bunk bed stood on each side of the door; each one had three tiers.

"You get the one at the bottom," he said, pointing to the bed to the left of the door. I could see that the bunk already had a blanket on it, as did the one just above me and the one on the bottom opposite mine.

"Considering what it was like in the barn, this is wonderful. A bed, a blanket and a latrine with running water, what else could I want in life? Do we also get free lice?" I asked.

"Yes, as much as you want, usually more," he answered.

"On the subject of everything I want, do we get steak too?" I asked with a grin on my face. In fact, Mr. Hitler's diet for the P.O.W.'s consisted of one cup of ersatz coffee and a slice of schwartzbrot for breakfast. The bread was a mixture of one part white flour, one part black flour, one part potato and one part sawdust. The coffee was bitter and usually cold. It was so bad that I used part of it to shave with, hoping it would keep the lice off my face.

For dinner we had various soups. We had soup made from boiled grass, soup made from boiled potato skins, (with the skin removed prior to giving it to us), and soup made from things not commonly thought of as food fit for human consumption. It was common to have bugs floating on top of the soup. We usually didn't get bread with dinner. I didn't mention lunch because there was no such thing, although I often used the little knife my dad had given me to cut my morning bread ration into quarters so I could nibble on it later in the day. Even so, I was hungry the entire time I was a P.O.W.. We all swore, many times, that we would steal and possibly kill before going that hungry again.

Top row: Bruno Galinski and Tex.
Bottom row: Alec Hurley a.k.a. The Minge, Trevor Evans, Sy Brenner,
and John Alberti.

On one occasion, when the Germans brought in a sack of lentils, we outsmarted ourselves. They told us to separate the little stones from the lentils; naturally, thinking that the lentils were meant for the Germans, we left mostly stones. But in fact the lentils were for us-the only decent meal the Krauts ever served us. So they had the last laugh as we broke our teeth on the rocks.

Little by little, over the next several days, I had chance to meet all of the medics in the Lazarett. It was quite an international group. There were Scots from Scotland, and Taffies from Wales, Paddies from Ireland and a Londoner whom the other Brits called the 'minge', which meant he was a homosexual. His real name was Alec Hurley. Among the patients, there were guys from all over the world as well. There were even Indians, the kind from India, who had been part of the Colonial Guard Troops. For the rest of the time I spent in Stalag V-A, I got along very well with the American medics.

The one I admired the most was Masa, the Japanese fellow. After the war, Masa sent me a picture of himself while he was in a hospital in Denver. He wrote a beautiful note on the reverse side, saying I was his inspiration. I'm sure that thought worked both ways. Another one who became a close companion was John Alberti, from Philadelphia. There were many more names that I just can't remember anymore. As you might guess from the looks on our faces in this picture, our morale was not always the greatest.

There is a unique bond that is created when men are placed together in a difficult situation and must work together.
Within the confines of the Lazarett, we grew to rely on each other and to respect one another.
We became friends.

CHAPTER 13

Day One in the Lazarett

A little later on that first day, I got a taste of what my life in the Lazarett would be like. I was looking out the window of the Verbandzimmer toward the camp when I heard a knock on the door. Turning, I saw a tall dark man walk in.

"Hi, I'm Bruno Galinski, one of the medics. I need to borrow your scissors so I can get a haircut," he said with a bright smile on his pockmarked face.

I laughed and said, "I don't have a scissors."

He replied, "Yes you do. They are in your tool box."

"I don't have a tool box," I said.

"Yes you do." He said pointing to my small sterilizer. "That's your tool box." We both laughed, and I knew right away he was my kind of guy and that we would become friends.

Bruno was a tall dark fellow with a warm smile on his face, but he looked as though he had been at the camp for some time because he had a very gaunt look about him. A hungry look.

"I'm a Polack from Chicago," he said grinning. "Where are you from?"

I was about to say that I was a Jew from Detroit, but kept that to myself. "I'm from Detroit."

"A kid from Detroit, huh?"

It was obvious that Bruno was much older than I. He was a gentleman and didn't have a foul mouth like Chris. He once told me he was going to own a bar when he got back to Chicago. He did. A few years after the end of the war, he sent me a postcard with the name of the bar, "The Raft."

I fished the scissors out of the sterilizer with a forceps and handed it to him. "Try to keep the lice off of it."

He laughed and said that he had made a deal with one of the Polish prisoners. "He said he was a barber before the war, anyway, he said he would cut my hair for a cigarette." Just as they were often the currency on the front line, cigarettes were the currency of the camp.

A short time later, two more medics came in carrying an American on a stretcher. The medic at the foot of the stretcher was a tall guy. He must have been six foot four inches tall and built like a linebacker. Sure enough, his name was Tex. Tex was from Mule Shoe, Texas. When he told me where he was from, I burst out laughing, and he said everyone responded the same way. He couldn't understand why. Poor Tex was assigned to the Lazarett, but he wasn't a medic. Because of his size, he was always given the grunt and dirty work, carrying guys up the stairs, cleaning up the latrines, washing floors and stuff like that. He always got the shit detail. He never had a smile on his face, but who could blame him?

As tall as Tex was, the other guy was short, even shorter than I was. From Philadelphia, John Alberti was the son of a Lutheran minister. He seemed like a nice guy but didn't have the outgoing personality that Bruno had. He was just a real quiet guy.

The patient was an American kid who looked like he was in a lot of pain. "I have frozen toes, Doc," he said with a grimace. "It hurts like hell."

Tex helped me remove the shoe on his left foot and the stench immediately nauseated me. I would have loved to open the window, as cold as it was, but it had been painted shut. The great toe was black and green. There was some crud oozing from under the toenail.

After looking at it, Paddy and I walked over to the door so the kid couldn't hear. We both agreed it had to come off. He could see I was queasy about doing this.

"He's one of yours, Yank," he said sarcastically. "You better do it before you have to take off the whole bloody leg." It occurred to me that Paddy might not be so brusque if he were in charge here; his resentfulness certainly wasn't much use to me now.

I poured some Kalen liquid-the only disinfectant we had-over the toe to clean the area, as if this might help. We didn't have anything to give the kid to help with the pain.

"Where are you from?" I asked, trying to ease the tension.

"Iowa," he answered, I could hear the fear in his voice.

"I'm not going to kid you about this. It's going to hurt, but we have to do it." I told him.

I could see he was afraid. Who wouldn't be? For some reason, he looked like he really trusted me. Why would he trust someone he didn't know when they said they had to cut off his toe? I was going to do something that would affect him for the rest of his life, and for some reason I couldn't understand, he trusted me to do the right thing. He didn't doubt me at all. I had enough doubts for the both of us.

I poured some Kalen on a dowel that already had plenty of teeth marks on it and told him to bite down on it. Unfortunately, the, "bite stick" was the only comfort we had to offer. I had John Alberti hold the other toes down away from the great toe so that I could get to the big one. Paddy handed me a large shears that resembled a pruning shears for trimming trees. That's what I did. I pruned his toe right off of his foot. It was mostly cartilage. There was very little bleeding. We then cleaned it again, put some cotton batting over the raw wound, and then wrapped it with the toilet paper. I kept wrapping the toilet paper around his foot and up around the ankle until his foot was a big white ball. There was no tape to hold the paper together, so I tucked the ends down.

The room was quiet other than the kid's whimpering. The other medics stared at me. I think they were impressed. When I put the shears down, I put my hands in my pants pockets so no one would see them shaking.

"No soccer for two weeks," I wisecracked to the kid as they started to lift him from the table.

Through the agony of his tears, he smiled briefly at my poor attempt at a joke as they carried him out the door. It was very quiet in the room for several minutes before anyone could say anything. The meaning of that moment stuck with me for the rest of my time in the camp, in fact for the rest of my life-humor really was good medicine. From now on, I made it a rule to try to make my patients laugh, or at least smile, as I dealt with their painful injuries. Although my jokes were usually pretty corny, I sure would like to think it helped!

The rest of the day was filled with more guys coming for treatment. As they started coming in, I felt like throwing up. First of all, there were no records on them, and we had nothing to keep records on. We didn't even know their names in most cases. It didn't take us long, however, to figure out who had captured our patients. The Wehrmacht, the regular German Army, treated their prisoners the way we did. They bandaged them properly, and if the wound required surgery it was done by our doctors. If men came in like they were from our Stalag, in other words, without proper care, we knew they had been captured by the, "SS-Hitler's prized cutthroats.

The one who got to me the most was a towheaded kid we all called Whitey. Of all the guys I saw that day, including the guy with the toe, Whitey was in the worst shape. It was apparent that he had been operated on in a field hospital, and his bone was exposed from just above the right knee all the way to the groin. All we could do was clean the area with Kalen, wrap the wound with cotton batting and wrap it with the toilet paper. It already smelled pretty bad. Whitey was sweating a lot, and he was very pale. He was in a lot of pain, but he was a gamer. Most of the guys were.

Thankfully, after Whitey, we were done for the day. Later, we went to our room for what we jokingly called dinner. After dinner, we sat on our bunks talking, getting to know each other. Bruno talked a lot about his wife. He talked about how he missed her. John talked about his girl back in Chicago, too. Other guys would come in and visit, everyone pretty much was in the same situation. Did our family know we were alive? Were they OK? Guys with wives or girls would wonder if they had found someone new. Pretty soon, there would be five or six guys sitting around crying. Even though I didn't have a special girl back home, I cried too.

I've never forgotten those long, very cold and very dark nights. As the guys would fall off to sleep, I would lay there with my thoughts. I would try to stay warm by curling up on my bunk wrapped in the one blanket. I would fold the top of the mattress over to use as a pillow. The bunks had only four or five slats underneath the lumpy mattress that was nothing more than a few scoops of hay covered with burlap. The cold would seep up from the bottom all night long. Still, this was better than that barn full of lice.

As I lay on my hard bunk that first night in the Lazarett, I had a vision of one of the loveliest experiences of my childhood: When I was about nine or ten years old, the Detroit Tigers baseball team was playing an exhibition game with the National League's Boston Braves. Admission was free, but every child who wanted to attend had to be accompanied by an adult. My mother came upon me crying in the kitchen of our home and asked me what was wrong. I explained the situation to her and she said, "What time is the game?" I said, "Today at three."

She astounded me when she said, "I'll take you." She put on her babushka and we went out and boarded the Trumble Street trolley, heading for Navin Field. This little old Jewish lady who didn't know anything about baseball took me to my first professional baseball game. When we got there we encountered an overflow crowd, but since it was an exhibition game, fans were allowed to stand on the outfield warning track, all the way from the right field corner to the left field corner. We were standing in center field. I remember how friendly was the Braves outfielder, Smead Jolly, who told us to watch it when the ball was coming our way. My mother stayed all nine innings and fought the crowds going home on the streetcar, never complaining. My brothers couldn't believe it. I know she did a lot of wonderful things for me as well as for others, but this is one kindness of hers that I'll never forget.

That first night I also thought about the people I had met and what had happened that day. Sleepless, I thought too, a lot about the last day I was at home. My mother and father had come to the railroad station to see me off. My brother Saul, drove them down for a tearful send off. It was very rough on my mother. My brother Myer, had already been gone for more than a year since he enlisted the day after Pearl Harbor and was in Hawaii.

Shivering from the cold, I really began to hate that Kraut who took my pipe from me. It used to keep my hands warm, even if we were stuck in foxholes in the snow.

Bruno's getting a haircut made me think back to when I was about 4 years old during the Depression. My Dad had a friend named Mickey Ratkin who was a barber. He would come to our house on Sunday mornings and give us all haircuts for twenty-five cents. Sometimes my father would get a haircut too.

Years later, when I was in high school, I stopped into a barber shop across from Central High School and sat myself into the barber's chair and looked out the window. The sign said, "Mickey's Barber Shop."

As I sat in the chair, this man with black hair and a mustache put his hand under my chin and said, "Little Seymour Brenner?" What a hell of a thing to think up while trying to fall asleep in the Lazarett at Stalag V-A. What a way to end my first day on the job!

While we were going through one of the small villages,
we were going at a fast pace. I heard that one of the
riflemen discovered a small jewelry store with jeweled
swastika stick pins in the window.
I had never seen anyone loot before, but the little store
was broken into.
The safe was blown and a lot of hoopla followed....

CHAPTER 14

Man of Confidence

About a week after I had arrived in the Lazarett, an American in the uniform of a Lieutenant Colonel came into the Verbandzimmer. Up until that day I hadn't seen any officers in the camp. By sheer reaction, I jumped up and yelled, "Sir."

He smiled and sat down on the stool next to the table. There was a small cut on his left forearm that needed a bandage. Looking at him, I noticed that he had two cigars sticking out of his shirt pocket. I became a little suspicious of him. He didn't have any insignia on him showing his branch of service. How did he come about having cigars in a place like this?

"I understand that you, being here in the Verbandzimmer, are the least bothered by the Germans," he said in a quiet voice.

I looked at him, puzzled, not knowing what to say.

"I mean, they don't come in here very often," he prompted, "They don't come snooping around to see what's going on here."

I continued to be suspicious. I had heard that the Germans had put spies in the camp. The other P.O.W.'s called them, 'plants' because they were planted there by the Krauts. They were Krauts who spoke English as well as we did, some of them even had lived in the States or in England. The French even told me that the French dentist down the hall should not be trusted. I had noticed that Alain, the French dentist and his partner, Armand, both had warmer clothes than the rest of us and looked very well fed. They were always talking quietly to each other and would shut up when someone else was around. The other Frenchies told me not to say anything to either of them that I didn't want the, "Boch" to hear; they figured that both of them were plants.

"Who are you?" I asked suspiciously. "How do I know you aren't a plant?"

"Good, you're careful. That's important. I'm going to tell you a secret," he said. "I'm with G-2. I don't have to tell you what would happen to me if the Germans found out about that."

I could see his point. I had heard that the Germans could get any information they wanted from you if they really tried. It wasn't pleasant how they did it, either. If this guy were really with Army Intelligence, he would have plenty of information they would want.

"Since the English doctor left, the Lazarett doesn't have an M.O.C.," he told me.

I didn't know what an M.O.C. was, so I asked him.

"Man of Confidence. The M.O.C. is appointed by the P.O.W.'s to speak for them. He goes to the Commandant with complaints. You don't have enough blankets, you don't get any mail, the food is poor, that kind of thing."

He went on to explain that the Germans, being the organized people that they were, even had an organized way the prisoners were to complain. They had one person who represented the prisoners. This way, the Germans didn't have to deal with too many people.

"I've decided to make you the M.O.C. for the Lazarett," he told me. "I spoke to the Commandant and he authorized it. I want you to complain about everything; Make his life miserable. Don't worry. You'll have plenty to complain about; you won't have to make things up. Get Henk Das to set up a meeting and in a very military-like way. You respectfully go to the Commandant with complaints or concerns. He hates problems like that, so we try to give him as many problems as we can."

The Colonel told me that he'd be coordinating with the M.O.C. from the Stalag. The other M.O.C. would see to it that I got word as to what the problems were on that side.

"Aren't you the M.O.C. in the camp?" I asked.

"They're transferring me out. They transfer me around a lot," he said matter-of-factly.

A few days later, a P-47 pilot who was shot down came into camp. The guys who caught him had taken his second lieutenant's bars, probably as a souvenir. I had Henk Das set up a meeting with the Commandant. I was very nervous walking into his office the next day. I could understand pretty much of what they were saying. I had to be very careful not to let them know.

Through Henk, I told the Commandant that I knew that the Germans respected rank in the Army, and that I respectfully requested that the Lieutenant be given back his bars.

The Commandant asked when the lieutenant had arrived, and I answered that he came into the Lazarett on Saturday. I listened to Henk translate this, but it sounded like he made a mistake. He had said, "Samstag."

Later when we were walking back to the Lazarett, I asked Henk what "Samstag" meant.

"Saturday," he answered.

That was when I realized how important it was for me not to try to speak German. How easy it would have been to make a fatal error using the Yiddish word for Saturday, "Shabbos," which also means "the Sabbath," instead of the correct German word, which I didn't even know! That was just one of the many differences between German and Yiddish. That mistake would be a dead, and I do mean dead, giveaway.

The next day, the Lieutenant had his bars back.

Suddenly, this little Jewish kid from Detroit wasn't such a kid. I started to think of myself as a man. I was humbled. I was also scared. They could still find out I was a Jew. These guys were depending on me. If the Krauts found out I was a Jew, I wouldn't be much good to anyone. I'd just be dead. I'd have to be more careful. I'd have to make sure I didn't speak until Henk translated for me, no matter how well I understood what was being said without his translation. Speaking Yiddish, and understanding German because of it, could help me, but it could also be the thing that gets me killed if I'm not careful.

When I returned from the Commandant's office, I had only one patient in the Verbandzimmer to see. Whitey was already lying on the table waiting for his daily dressing change. I knew it was Whitey before I looked at him, I always knew from the smell coming from his wound. Every wound had its own smell, but none of them smelled as bad as Whitey's. As I went to work on his dressing, I had trouble pulling the cotton away from the bone, it had been saturated with the crud that had been draining and was now dried up. I was afraid that if I pulled it off, it would make the wound worse. If I didn't pull it off, it would make the wound worse. I looked at Whitey's face to see if he was in a lot of pain, but as usual, he was biting his lower lip and staring at the ceiling over the door. He didn't want to make me feel bad about hurting him.

I wanted to cry, but I didn't want him to feel badly, so I started singing, "See that man, standing over there, he picks his nose and flings it in the air..."

I poured some kalen on the old dressing to loosen it up and gently pulled it away. I poured some more to clean out the wound and stuffed more cotton into the wound and wrapped it with the toilet paper.

Later that night, after what we laughingly called dinner, we were sitting on our bunks talking. We were freezing and hungry. Alberti was worried. His girl probably thinks he is dead; she probably has a new boyfriend. Bruno is worried about his family. Guys would come into our room to shoot the bull, but nobody really felt like talking. There was just too much tension in the room. I started telling jokes. I don't know why, but that's what I do. If an English guy walked in the room, I talked with an English accent. If a French guy came in, I spoke with a French accent. When the Scotties came in, I'd come in with a loud Scotch Brogue.

"As they say in Scotland, Laddie, a lad was walking down the lane and as he walked beside a little Lassie, he said, 'hello there lassie,'" I rolled the 'r' in exaggeration of their speech,

"May I walk beside you Lassie?" Said he.

And she said, "Aye Laddie, aye."

And he said, would you like to sit on the park bench with me Lassie?"

And she said, "Aye Laddie Aye."

Then he asked, "May I put me arm abooot you Lassie?"

And she said, "Aye Laddie, aye."

He then asked, "May I give you a wee little kiss?"

And she said, "Nay, Laddie, nay."

He asked, "What is the matter, Lass? Do you not like the gleam in me eye?"

And she answered, "Nay, Laddie, nay, 'Tis not the gleam in your eye, 'tis the tilt in your kilt".

Bruno was talking about his wife, and Alberti was talking about his girlfriend. He said he had met his girl in high school, but other than that, he had hated high school.

I said I had a lot of fun in high school. I graduated from Northern High School in Detroit and had a lot of great memories. I had been a member of the radio club, I had the lead in the senior play, and I was the catcher on the school baseball team. I was even named the most talented boy in my graduating class.

I met my first real girlfriend, Celia, when she had the lead, opposite me in the senior play. She was a very sweet girl and was my prom date.

As I finished talking about high school, the door opened and in walked Chris, the Jew Hater from basic training.

He said, "Hi guys, I'm your new roommate."

Whenever I had to call on the camp Commandant in my role as Man-of-Confidence-in other words, to complain on behalf of the patients whose most basic needs went unmet-it seemed he always had a cigar in his mouth. When I unleashed my complaint, his eyes looked to the ceiling, as if he were thinking deeply before answering me. Sometimes, he would take the cigar from his mouth and roll it round in his fingers, then replace it. Finally, he would reply. His apparent thoughtfulness never failed to impress me; I was quite sure he was putting his mind in gear before he put his mouth in motion.

I remembered this little affectation for the rest of my life, and generally tried to emulate him (without the cigar) whenever any knotty problem emerged in business or at home that required my attention.

CHAPTER 15

Chris

In an instant, I felt my world start to collapse. I felt like a bowl of jelly. The last person in the world I wanted to meet again was Erwin Chrzanowski. I could see so clearly in my memory our fight back in basic, and the hatred in his eyes. Here I was in a position where all he had to do was make one small remark to a guard, or even to one of the other prisoners, and my life would be finished.

In my mind, I felt that the best way for me to stay alive was to try to repair my relationship with him. If he felt that his time in the Lazarett would be better with me as a friend, he might not say anything.

All these thoughts occurred in the first instant it took for him to look down at me and recognize that he knew someone in the room.

"Oh, you're here too," he said, standing in the doorway. His arms were wrapped around his body with his hands tucked into the armpits to keep warm.

I stood up and feeling very awkward, shook his hand. "This is Chrzanowski," I said without looking away from him.

Bruno stood up to shake his hand, saying, "Great, another Polack, I'm Bruno Galinski and this is John Alberti." He pointed to Alberti in the upper bunk above his. Chris didn't seem to like being called a Polack but he didn't say anything.

While it was true that they both had Polish blood, Bruno and Chris were as different as two people could be. Bruno was well mannered and quite bright, while Chris was a crude, loud anti-Semite.

"Chris and I were in the same outfit from the day we started basic," I said. Then, trying to show some concern I asked, "Didn't you get a blanket when they told you to come up here?"

"No," he said, "and I was afraid to ask them anything. They don't seem very friendly."

"I'll help you," I said.

"Yeah, he's the M.O.C., he can get you a blanket if anyone can," Bruno said this with obvious admiration that I held such an important position in the Lazarett. "He'll tell you some good jokes too."

As we walked down the stairs, I told him what the M.O.C. was.

"I'm the man to come to if you have a problem. I'll do anything I can to help you." I wanted him to feel that he needed my friendship.

"There are two guards who keep an eye on us," I explained, "One of them is nice and the other one is a real asshole. The nice one is from England. We call him Johnny. He was visiting his family here in Germany when the war started, and they wouldn't let him go home. He got drafted and was placed here to guard the prisoners. He's a pretty nice guy. The other guard for the Lazarett is a real mean S.O.B. we call, "Little Caesar." He likes to beat on the prisoners, so try to stay away from him if you can. You'll see him in the morning. He comes in to wake us up, and he's not very gentle about how he does it. Johnny is usually around at night, so I shouldn't have a problem getting you a blanket.

When we got back upstairs with his blanket, the other guys were already asleep. I told him he should take the bunk above mine, saying, "This is sure a lot better than that barn."

He nodded agreement, climbing up above. Not wanting to wake the others, we didn't say anymore that night. I rolled up the top part of the burlap mattress to use as a pillow. I usually spent those frozen dark nights thinking of my family and friends back home, but that night, I could only lay there in fear thinking about all the things that could go wrong with Chris there. Maybe it was "Beshert".

I never quite understood what Chris was doing among us during his three months or so in the Lazarett. I didn't even know what his job was. Each night he was with us, I went to sleep in fear and woke up in fear, expecting the guards to arrive any minute to take away the Jew. This was an especially nervous period for me. But he never said anything.

Not long after Easter, Chris disappeared in the middle of the night. I received a message from him the next morning, in which he told me he'd appreciate it if I brought him his jacket and a few personal articles, since he was freezing. I went over to the main camp on the pretense of making a sick call. I wore his jacket and carried a small bag with a half a slice of bread in it along with a few other things. When he saw me, he shook my hand warmly and took his goods, and that was the last I ever saw of him. As long as he had been anywhere in my vicinity, I felt like I was sitting on a time bomb that could go off at any second. Once, even later, I heard that Chris was part of a group that was forced to march to another Stalag; many of the men on the march died or disappeared. I guess I was the lucky one again.

I heard a lot of men crying. As a medic, I saw them in great pain. Some would groan in anguish and a lot unashamedly would pray aloud in many languages. Some would scream,
"Please don't cut my leg off."
Legs, arms, it was all a nightmare. I was in the middle of it.

CHAPTER 16

Christmas

The next morning, I could hardly keep my eyes open. I doubt that I got any sleep at all. It wouldn't take much for Chris to let someone know I was a Jew and my life would be over. What if he talked to the guards? What if he talked to one of the plants? What if they came in the middle of the night and I disappeared, just like others I had heard about. My mind was overloaded with, "what ifs" the whole night.

The Verbandzimmer was pretty busy that morning. There had been several new prisoners brought in the night before, and many had untreated wounds. Fortunately, most of them weren't serious.

Once when I stepped out into the hall to look for someone to help move some stretchers, I noticed a man curled up on the floor in a prenatal position, sucking his thumb. Something had to be done to improve the situation, but what?

Masa had told me about this. Guys just seemed to give up. They didn't have any desire to live anymore. He told me that once they reached the point that this guy was in, having lost the spirit to live, they usually died. There had been several like this in the last week.

One of the new P.O.W.'s was complaining about Christmas. He said that Christmas meant a lot to him. His buddies in his unit were going to have a Christmas party, and now he wouldn't have a Christmas. That was when it came to me. I knew we could boost morale by putting on a Christmas show. After seeing how easy it was for me to get the bars back for that lieutenant, I thought I would go and test my luck with the Commandant again.

I arranged with Henk to go with me to see him. While standing there listening to them speak, I heard the Commandant tell Henk that I had a very nice voice. He asked what I did before the war. I almost answered before Henk translated the question to me but caught myself at the last minute. After Henk asked me in English, I looked at the Commandant and told him I had been a radio announcer.

"Ah, ja, gut, radio shprochen, ja gut," he said, smiling at me, tilting his head as if he knew it all the time.

I hoped he did not compare notes with the Feldwebel. I had told him I was an ambulance driver.

Not only did the Commandant allow us to have a Christmas show, he even furnished us with a violinist and a pianist. The two musicians turned out to be doctors, French and Polish, but I don't remember which played which instrument.

If the Commandant could provide us with physicians to help with musical entertainment, perhaps I could persuade him to let us have them when we needed them to care for our patients. I had just the patient in mind, too, Whitey. I was determined to ask once the party was over. It might be the only way to help him.

The party was held on the third floor of the Lazarett. It was mainly used for extra barracks when needed, but they never needed it. The prisoners were not supposed to go up there, and until the Christmas party, we hadn't been up there. It was one large room that went from one end of the building to the other.

All the patients who were not ambulatory were taken upstairs by the medics with the help of the patients who were ambulatory. I made sure there was a place for Whitey right up front.

I was the emcee of the show and had a great time cutting up, telling jokes, making fun of our situation and of our captors as well. My goal was to get everyone in a happy festive mood, ready for the show. Once I had everyone laughing, I introduced the first act.

"And now from that little island off the coast of New Zealand, I give you the Canberra Can Can Quadrille!" I said in my deepest announcer's voice.

Three burly bewhiskered Australians came up with blankets wrapped around their middles doing the Can Can, flashing their hairy legs and arms. At the end of their routine, they turned around and lifted the back of their blankets, mooning the audience. It was hysterical.

Everyone got into the act, and we all had a great time. I think I had a better time than anyone else did, announcing each act with a joke or two. I think I used every accent and dialect I knew.

The Germans did something very unexpected. During the performance, Johnny came up and told three guys to come with him for a work detail. They were not very happy about that, being called away from the party, but knew better then to argue with the guards; even a nice one like Johnny. When they came back, they brought our Red Cross packages. The Swiss had arranged for the P.O.W.'s to get packages every month, but, usually the Krauts kept them for themselves. They would keep them or give them to the women in town in exchange for a good time.

The two doctors played a duet of Christmas songs, and I really embarrassed myself when I started to announce the next act. They totally ignored me and started to play their next selection. They both had very serious looks on their faces the entire time.

I told a joke that was a parody of American cigarette commercials, but the Americans were the only ones who understood it. The British sang a lot of songs popular, in England and the Americans sang a song called, "Don't Fence Me In," which seemed very appropriate for our situation. The two most popular songs were, "Roll Me Over in the Clover" and, "Three Old Maids Locked in the Lavatory." It went like this:

Oh, say, what can the matter be?

Three old maids locked in the lavat'ry.

They were there from Monday to Saturday.

Nobody knew they were there.

The men kept singing that song over and over again long after the party as just a distant memory. I ended the show with this last joke.

As I was standing guard in front of the orderly room with an empty .45 strapped to my belt, I heard voices in the orderly room, and it sounded like they were arguing. One said we'll leave it up to the man who is charge of quarters, and the other one said, "OK."

They came out, and I snapped to attention as a bird colonel said to me that he would like me to settle a little argument that he and the general were having.

I said, "Sir, I do not want to get involved", but the General said that they just wanted an honest answer.

"You won't have any negative repercussions no matter what you answer", the General went on. "I say that intercourse is 50% work and 50% pleasure and the Colonel says that it is 100% pleasure. What do you think?"

I said, "Sir, I think its 100% pleasure because if there was any work involved, you would have me doing it."

They say that memories are made so that we can smell the roses in December, but my memories were wilted in the spring of my life.
We were stripped of our humility.
We were treated inhumanely.
We were Prisoners of War.

CHAPTER 17

The French

December 28, 1944

Whitey's leg was getting worse. The stench from his wounds had gotten so bad as to make me nauseated when I had to change his dressings. I realized we were not going to be able to save his leg if we didn't get things turned around soon. I just didn't have the knowledge to care for him properly.

We had been so busy with other things; I hadn't given his problem the attention I should have. I was feeling overloaded. On the one hand, I had to care for all these injuries; on the other, I had to deal with the Commandant. I admonished myself for not having done more for poor Whitey.

Tex and Alberti worked together as a team, moving patients from place to place and helping out in any way they were asked. I only saw them once in a while. It was comical seeing them together. Tex was six foot four and Alberti was five foot seven. I called them, "The long of it and the short of it."

As the long of it and the short of it were taking Whitey back to his room, a French officer walked into the Verbandzimmer. He was a short, trim, very neatly dressed clean-shaven man. He walked up to me and offered his well-manicured hand to shake. His grip was surprisingly slight as he offered a quiet, "Comment ça va? (How are you?)." This was the usual friendly greeting the French gave, but they usually had a much firmer grip than he did. His voice was very soft. He wore wire-rimmed glasses on his gaunt face. His uniform was clean and even looked neat and pressed which was very unusual for a P.O.W.. His English was very good and easy to understand. He certainly didn't look like your average French P.O.W..

He got right to the point. "My name is Alphonse de la Haye. I am the head of the French Committee. We have organized the French men in the camp and the Lazarett. We are having a problem finding a place to meet that the Boch would not find out about. It seems that your Verbandzimmer is, for some reason, above suspicion."

Interesting, I thought to myself, he used almost the exact same words as that Lieutenant Colonel who made me M.O.C..

This was true. The guards never came in or bothered us in any way while we were in that room.

That first meeting was very brief, but the gist of it was that Alphonse was the head of the French Underground, and that they wanted to meet with me. It seemed that the only safe place to meet was in my Verbandzimmer.

After I agreed to meet with them, he said one more thing. "Monsieur Brenner, please understand that it would be best if you did not discuss this with anyone else. The dentist, Alain, and the fat one, Armand, did you ever notice how well fed and healthy they look? We do not trust them. I'm sure you will understand this."

"Until we meet again, Monsieur," he said, and he offered his hand to me again with another "Ça va?" Life in the Lazarett was sure getting complicated.

Armand is on the left and Alain, the dentist, is on the right.

We weren't getting many English P.O.W.'s in the Verbandzimmer. Paddy didn't come very often. He did come in from time-to-time to help me clean up or to help with guys who had more serious wounds. There were a few new P.O.W.'s who were amputees and needed new dressings on their stumps. Often, their wounds would be draining and would need cleaning and pressure dressings. Usually, guys like that were not in the Lazarett for more than a few days before they were moved somewhere else, and we never saw them again. I was kept pretty busy and was appreciative with the help Paddy gave, but we still didn't talk much.

Men who were prisoners of war rarely talked about women; they talked about food. One evening, a group of us sat around in the Verbandzimmer, shooting the bull as we used to say, and talking about food, naturally.

I said, "Boy, if I were home, I would jump in the car and go down to my favorite restaurant, Lellie's. I'd have a big steak, about so big," and I'd spread my hands out wider than a normal plate.

Paddy exploded, madder than hell, shouting at the top of his voice, "You Yanks, all you can talk about is your damn big steaks and your big cars."

That's when I let him have it. I told him, "If you English weren't so stupid you could have big steaks and big cars, too if you built some roads and if you really set your minds to it you could have indoor plumbing."

That shut him up for a while.

A P.O.W. was a man who suffered inhumane treatment all day, every day. He was humiliated and stripped of his dignity. The fact that we worked in the Lazarett didn't make any difference in how we were treated. Most of the guys across the road in the camp didn't have anything to occupy their time, and so they would dwell on the inhumane treatment. It was probably a blessing that we were as busy as we were. We didn't always have time to think about it; but it still happened.

CHAPTER 18

Sadistic Treatment

While some of the camp guards were probably no different than anyone else and were stuck there in a difficult situation, others were really sadistic and enjoyed humiliating the P.O.W.'s. The worst of the guards in the Lazarett was the one we called Little Caesar. He made it his goal in life to give us as much grief as possible. We hung that nickname on him because of his odd appearance: He looked more Italian than German, what with his short, stocky build and his swarthy complexion. He slicked his hair back with some greasy goop-it could have been olive oil for all we knew. Most of all though, the Little Caesar tag fit his Nazi demeanor. While his eyes scowled at us, he always wore a menacing grin that reminded us of the evil gangster character played by Edgar G. Robinson. He never let up, goading us kriegies relentlessly, and he truly seemed to enjoy it.

After a busy morning working in the Verbandzimmer, Little Caesar came up with Henk Das to translate and ordered everyone, including all the patients, outside into the freezing weather. "He said we were not getting enough exercise," groaned Henk. While we didn't have heat in our rooms, the heat from the guard's rooms down stairs would rise enough to make life on the second floor bearable. Outside was the coldest winter in European history. I told him it was not possible to take the sick patients outside in the freezing weather. Little Caesar just smiled sadistically at me as Henk translated back that he wasn't asking me for advice.

Once outside in the area between the fence and the buildings, we were shown that the tops from tin cans had been thrown around the area. It was obvious that he had poured water on them so that they would freeze there in the ground. He ordered us to get down on our hands and knees and to pick them up off the frozen ground.

"Mach schnell," he would scream, walking around, hitting us in the backs of our shoulders or in the head with his rifle butt.

In no time at all, guy's fingers were bleeding, skin scrapped away and frozen from the cold.

I snuck the little knife my father had given me out from the lining of my pants and hid it under my thumb. I was able to use it to pry the lids out of the ground without injuring my fingers.

By the time we were let back into the Lazarett, we were all freezing, and I was one of the few who didn't have to have bandages placed on my fingers or knees. Some of the men had cuts on the back of their heads from being hit with the rifle. Caesar went out of his way to be as mean to the new arrivals as possible.

The guards were constantly telling us that the war was almost over, that they were kicking the Allies back across the Channel. It wasn't hard to believe, considering the large numbers of P.O.W.'s they were sending, but the P.O.W.'s were telling a different story.

I spoke to Henk and told him I needed to talk to the Commandant about this treatment. The way it worked was that I would contact Henk, he would talk to the Feldwebel, and the Feldwebel would arrange it with the Commandant. It didn't work that way this time.

Henk said that the Feldwebel wouldn't listen to my demands.

"He said that the Commandant knew everything that went on in the Lazarett and would see no one."

I then asked to see the Commandant again, this time to request better sanitary conditions, better food for the wounded and replacement light bulbs for the Verbandzimmer. This time, the Feldwebel told Henk that I should be grateful that they allowed us to have music and a Christmas party. He said we should appreciate the wonderful food we got from the Red Cross packages we received at Christmas.

I said that we were supposed to get the packages every month and that we received one package for four men when we were supposed to receive a package for each man. The Feldwebel smiled at me and laughed.

ONE PER WEEK PER MAN

RED   CROSS

BRITISH		AMERICAN		CANADIAN	
Condensed Milk	1 can	Powdered Milk-16oz.	1 can	Powdered Milk	1 can
Meat Roll	1 can	Spam	1 can	Spam	1 can
Meat & Vegetable	1 can	Corned Beef	1 can	Corned Beef	1 can
Vegetable or Bacon	1 can	Liver Paste	1 can	Salmon	1 can
Sardines	1 can	Salmon	1 can	Cheese-8 Oz.	1 can
Cheese-4 oz.	1 can	Cheese	1 can	Butter-16 oz.	1 can
Margarine or Butter	1 8oz.	Margarine-16 oz.		Biscuits-soda	1 box
Biscuits	1 pkg.	Biscuits--K-Ration		Coffee-ground-8 oz.	1 bag
Eggs-Dry	1 can	Nescafe Coffee-4 oz.	1 can	Jam	1 can
Oatmeal	1 can	Jam or Orange Pres.	1 can	Prunes-8 oz.	1 box
Cocoa	1 can	Prunes or Raisins	1 can	Raisins-8 oz.	1 box
Tea-2 oz.	1 box	Sugar-8oz.	1 box	Sugar-8 oz.	1 bag
Dried Fruit or Pudding	1 can	Chocolate-4oz.	2 bars	Chocolate-5 oz.	1 bar
Sugar-4 oz.	1 box	Soap	2 bars	Soap	1 bar
Chocolate	1 bar	Cigarettes	5 pks.		
Soap	1 bar				

REICH ISSUE

WEEKLY RATION

Army Bread-1 loaf	2100 grams	Soup-Oatmeal, Barley or Pea	3 times
Vegetables-Potatoes	400 grams	Cheese	46 grams
Other Seasonal	?	Sugar	175 grams
Jam	175 grams	Mare	215 grams
Meat		Salt	
Flour---on occasion			

Food Parcel

It was one of those situations that P.O.W.'s face all the time. No matter what I said, he wasn't going to let me speak to the Commandant.

After the Feldwebel left, Henk told me that he thought that the Feldwebel felt threatened by the fact that the Commandant listened to me. Das went on to say that it was possible that the Commandant didn't know about the beatings and that he would be angry with the Feldwebel for allowing it to happen.

The next morning, Alphonse the mysterious Frenchman showed up with a French soldier who had been wounded in the shoulder. He was an ordinary looking guy in his early thirties, not especially handsome, but well built and rugged, with a serious look on his face. He seemed happy to meet me and his facial expressions and body language suggested to me that he might turn out to be a good friend and ally.

Once I cleaned the area around his wound, I could see that there was a shell fragment, probably from a grenade, sticking out of it. Because of the poor quality of the materials we worked with, the wounds would start bleeding every time we changed the dressing. With this patient, I applied the dressing differently. I don't know what made me think of it, but I soaked the cotton with the kalen and put it over the wound. I then covered the wet cotton with some dry cotton and wrapped the toilet paper around several times to hold it in place. Then, I took a strand of toilet paper and twisted it into a long rope and tied it around the wound with the knot over the wound itself. I repeated this with a second rope of toilet paper and tied it below the first one. I decided to call it a, "wet dressing."

Most of the French wounded were taken to Alain and Armand down the hall. I assumed that Alphonse didn't want them to see this guy.

As they left, Alphonse said, "Merci beaucoup, my friend. It would be best if no one knew about our friend here." He nodded towards the wounded soldier. "I'm sure you understand."

Before they went out the door, he looked quickly down the hall to make sure no one was looking, and then led the man out the door.

My new wet dressing seemed to work well. I could change the dressings without causing the wounds to open up again.

I thought that this would probably be a good thing to try on Whitey, and as if on cue, Whitey was the very next patient to be brought in the door. Tex and Alberti both had worried looks on their faces.

"His temp is way up, and the wound smells even worse than before," said Alberti.

I had some trouble pulling the cotton away from the bone. The bone was exposed for about eight inches and the area around the wound both top and bottom was gray and secreting an alarming volume of pus. I knew there was no way we could save his leg. We were just fooling ourselves thinking we could. If we didn't take his leg soon, the infection could spread and he could die. He was such a brave guy, he put up with so much pain that we didn't always know how much pain he was in. I had to do something.

"Get Henk Das back in here," I told Tex.

He was there within minutes. I walked him out into the hall.

"Get that Feldwebel back here now. Right now," I yelled.

He was there within a few minutes with a pissed look on his face, but he wasn't prepared for the rage coming from me.

"If you don't let me talk to the Commandant, it's going to be your ass," I said pointing my finger hard into his chest. "This man needs a doctor, and he needs one now. The Commandant is responsible for getting him one. Go get him," I yelled at him, waving my hands at him, dismissing him to leave, and pushing him toward the stairs.

Henk tried to translate and he was just as mad as I was. The Feldwebel couldn't get down those stairs fast enough.

I kept yelling and Henk kept translating, "The Commandant is responsible for getting a doctor up here to help with this patient. We need him right now!"

"The Commandant is responsible for the health and care of every man in this Lazarett. If Whitey dies it will be his fault. You better make sure he knows. This man needs a doctor, and he needs one now. Not tomorrow, now. Go tell him," I yelled, waving my hand dismissing him to leave. I couldn't believe my audacity.

Everyone around me stared at me in disbelief that I would have the stones to yell at the Kraut like that. I couldn't believe it myself.

Out of the corner of my eye, I could see Alphonse down the hall watching me. He was smiling. I guess he approved.

The Commandant

Within the hour, I was summoned to the Commandant's office, and he received me in a military manner, clicking his heels and saluting. He politely asked, "What can I do for you?"

I told him that I had a man whose leg needed to be amputated. "That is something I cannot take the responsibility for doing myself. He must have a doctor."

His response surprised me. Without an argument, he said that a doctor would be at the Lazarett as soon as possible.

I felt that seeing that he was in such a giving mood, this was an opportune time to get additional supplies and possibly even larger light bulbs.

He replied to me that medical supplies come from the, 'Krankenhaus' (hospital), and he had no jurisdiction over them. He did say that larger light bulbs are not allowed.

"I will give you papers to allow you to go under guard to the Krankenhaus yourself and see if you can get what you need," he said, turning to his clerk and telling him to make out the necessary orders to let me go to the Krankenhaus. Henk told me that the clerk would send the orders over to me when they were ready.

The Doctor

The next morning, one of the doctors who had been at the Christmas party, was brought up to the Verbandzimmer. He had been very quiet at the Christmas party but now he seemed like a different person, immediately taking control of the situation. The trouble was that I didn't understand a word of what he was saying. He was speaking in Polish. Thank God that Henk Das was there to translate.

I had assumed that we would do the surgery in the Verbandzimmer because it had all of my supplies and the most light, due to the windows. Dr. Wroznotofski decided that the Verbandzimmer had too much traffic, too many people coming in and out, and would not be possible to keep it clean enough for the surgery. He really wanted to have a sterile place to do the operation. I didn't know how realistic that idea, was but he was the doctor. He decided on a small room at the opposite end of the hall. It had a very old 25-watt bulb with a huge filament in it. There was one small window on the outside wall opposite the door.

He said he planned to do the operation in two days, as he needed time to get some supplies for the operation. He told me to have the floors, the walls and window scrubbed, and I put Tex in charge of the cleaning details.

Then without so much as a word goodbye, Dr. Wroznotofski was off, waddling down the hall toward the stairway.

Now it was up to me to tell Whitey.

Being in a P.O.W. camp was a nerve-racking experience. Aside from being demoralized, having poor food and sanitation, having your masculinity taken away from you and having a generally hopeless feeling, you were also subject to constant fear. Everyone had nightmares and restful sleep rarely happened. Deep down in everyone's mind was the thought that we never knew if one day we would be lined up and shot or just disappear into the night. The possibility was always there.

The possibility was real.

CHAPTER 19

Our Hero: Masa

There were P.O.W.'s from all over the world in the Lazarett. Aside from Paddy's outbursts, we all got along pretty well. Still, guys tended to hang out with guys from their own country.

Men could, it seemed, disappear even in the light of day, as almost happened right before our eyes one cold afternoon in February. On this occasion, Masa Uchimura emerged from his obscurity to show his true colors as a heroic individual. I was in my Verbandzimmer that afternoon, when I suddenly heard the familiar sound of hobnail boots pounding up the stairs and then moving down the hall, stopping somewhere in the vicinity of Masa's, "ward of the unwanted."

A great hubbub from Masa's room filled the hall-the screech of a bunk or table being dragged across the floor, raised voices, objects of various sizes falling off shelves, and more. Looking through my doorway and down the corridor, I saw two German soldiers picking up some of the pneumonia patients, and none too gently. "Raus! Raus!" They yelled, as the sick soldiers scrambled to get to their feet with what little strength they could muster. As I edged closer to the ugly scene, I saw that the tuberculosis patients were having an even harder time, immobilized as they were by the suction-cup devices Masa had attached to their chests as part of their treatment.

I had no idea why the Germans were trying to roust these patients out. Was it another attempt to kill them with some kind of barbaric forced labor, outside in the freezing cold? How else could I explain it? The guards were holding up one TB patient by the arms--Tom Morgan-when Masa intervened. [1]

Before any of the sick men actually exited into the hall, Masa-looking much bigger than he really was-blocked the entire doorway with his body. Hands braced high on the doorjambs and his feet spread across the threshold, he was a sight to behold! He was white-hot mad, with all the veins on his forehead and neck bulging out in relief, thick as half-inch ropes. He shouted, "This is murder!" By now, all the doorways down the corridor, right and left, had filled up with curious spectators. No one could believe that the soft-spoken, nearly invisible Masa could take such a stance or raise his voice to such a pitch. "If you take these men out of here, that's murder! I'm going to have you prosecuted for murder!" He screamed.

Alphonse, with an expression of amazement spread across his face, saw this from his doorway. He made a gesture toward Masa, clapping his hands over his head, as if he were offering him a standing ovation for his outstanding performance.

After a tense moment, the German soldiers looked at Masa, then at each other. With defiant expressions on their faces, but clearly submissive body language, they shrugged their shoulders and then dropped the men back down in their bunks. Masa stepped aside as the Germans brushed past him and left. Everyone was stunned, as I'm sure Masa was himself. All of us in the Verbandzimmer looked at our Japanese American friend with a new sense of respect after that. Who knew that our unassuming Masa had it in him to be such a hero?

1   Tom Morgan came from Oakland, California. He had joined the Army in 1943, right out of high school. When wounded, he was attached to Company K, 397th Infantry Regiment, 100th Division. Morgan in fact had pleurisy and not TB, a common misdiagnosis, as we found out later. He maintained contact with Masa for many years after the war, and lives to this day in Walnut Creek, California.

Aussie Tea

There was comfort being with people who spoke your language and had similar background and culture. It gave you a feeling of comfort; a feeling of home, to talk about things that were familiar, things you could share with other people who were familiar with them. It was comfortable for an American to talk about baseball. It was comfortable for an Australian to talk about "football," but, their football wasn't the same as ours. It just didn't have that same comfortable feeling talking to them about these things. Each nationality had its own interests. Each nationality had its own music. The things that gave them comfort weren't the same things that gave us comfort.

So, we tended to hang out with our own countrymen. Still, I was fascinated listening to them talk about what their life was like before the war. It was like traveling around the world while staying in one place. As I got to know them better, I felt more and more comfortable with them, and they, I think, felt more comfortable with me.

I started to spend a lot of time with the Aussies. They were a wild bunch of guys who loved to tell jokes and loved to listen to mine. I was particularly honored when they invited me to join them in their daily tea ritual. They said they invited me because they enjoyed my stories, but never knew when to take me seriously. To this day, people still have that problem.

Every afternoon at 4:00 p.m., they would get together with the English and New Zealanders to have tea. It was their social event of the day. All in all, there were about ten guys. The problem was that they only had one tea bag. One, very old, very used, very important tea bag that was left over from one of the Red Cross parcels from Christmas. It was the last tea bag left. They would pour the hot water in each man's cup and then dunk the tea bag into the cup a few times. It didn't really do anything, but the ritual was everything to them.

Now, everyone knows that to make tea you need hot water. Each day, two guys would take their turn providing the hot water. This was not an easy task. When my turn arrived, Trevor Evans told me that he and I were assigned the important responsibility of getting the hot water. Everybody called Trevor , "Taffy", because he was from Wales. I never knew why people from Wales were called Taffy and he didn't explain it to me. He did teach me how to make the tea.

"Now, listen carefully, Laddie," he started, "To make a proper pot of tea, you need to have furiously boiling water. That's our task today, to get the water."

"How are we going to do that?" I asked. We don't have a fire here or a tea pot or anything."

"Just follow me and watch carefully," he answered with a twinkle in his eye.

He got a number 10 can[2] from under his bed and took it to the latrine at the end of the hall and filled it with water. We then went into my Verbandzimmer. The Verbandzimmer was the only room that had an electrical outlet. He placed the can on the wooden counter below the outlet and wrapped a wire hanger around the can, then bent the ends of the wire to point out. He then, using a towel, pushed the ends of the wire into the electrical outlet. I was terrified that he would electrocute himself, but nothing happened. He told me to wait until the water was furiously boiling, and then unplug the can and bring it into his room.

Feeling very honored at being given this important assignment, I waited until the water started bubbling. It seemed to take quite a long time, and I was worried they would think I was taking too long to get their water. As soon as I saw the water start to bubble, I got my jacket to wrap around the can so I could pull it away from the wall without burning my hands. The hanger easily pulled out of the outlet and I marched proudly down the hall to where they were waiting with their canteen cups.

After I put it down so they could pour it in their cups, they were obviously upset with me. I couldn't understand what was wrong. Had I taken too long?

"What's wrong?" I asked meekly, looking at their scornful faces,

Taffy answered angrily, "It has to be Furiously boiling, furiously, furiously, furiously boiling!" He proclaimed. "Didn't I tell you that, weren't you listening to me?"

"Damn Yanks," I heard from the corner. Without looking up, I knew who had said that.

Since we didn't have the light on in the room, we didn't notice that the act of boiling the water had also blown out the fuse and there was no electricity in the whole building.

About a half hour later, Johnny came upstairs from the guard's room and asked if any of the P.O.W.'s was an electrician.

We all started laughing, and he just looked at us puzzled. One of the guys suggested, "Get a bigger light bulb." Another guy told him, "Stick your finger in it."

"Call the Fuehrer; he should know bloody hell what to do." Laughed Taffy.

Then, I told him that maybe he should get a new fuse. I was laughing so hard when I told him, I don't think he took me seriously, even though that was what he really needed to do. Like everyone else, he just didn't know when to take me seriously.

After the tea ceremony, I went back to the Verbandzimmer to make sure I had the supplies I would need for the next day. When I walked in, I was surprised to see my new friend, Alphonse, leaning against the counter. Sitting on the bandage table, was another Frenchman with his arm in a sling.

---

2   A large tin can, a little larger then a two-pound coffee can, found in red cross parcels that were supposed to be delivered to the British soldiers. The Germans usually kept these packages for themselves.

"Good evening my friend." Said Alphonse, "I wonder if you could take a look at my friend's arm."

I realized this was more than just a request to change a bandage from the look on his face. I quietly closed the door. It was very rare that I would close the door, and I hoped that it wouldn't cause anyone to be suspicious. When I approached the man with the sling, he stood up and took off the sling, and I noticed that there wasn't any wound at all.

"Do you remember my friend, the soldier that you took care of the other day?" He asked.

"Sure, how is he?" I asked in return.

"Well he died, you see. We would like you to be in the honor guard at the funeral."

I looked at him amazed. He just had a little flesh wound; nothing that would cause him to die. Even with my little bit of training, I was sure of that.

"Don't misunderstand me," he said very quietly, approaching me so he could talk without anyone outside overhearing. "He isn't really dead. When we need to get someone out of the camp, we have him die. The box will be empty, except for some stones to give it weight, but the guards will think he is dead, and so they won't be asking about him at appelle (roll call)."

"Yes, but how do you get him out of camp?" I asked.

"He participates in the burial, then walks away while we distract the guard who is watching. It works quite well. We have done it before. There is another thing I want to ask you. I'd like to get a picture of you, if that is OK, for a souvenir."

He stood next to me with his arm around my shoulder as the other man took a camera out from where he had it hidden in his sling. He was about to take our picture when the door opened and Taffy stuck his head in. I was about to panic. I knew that the French didn't want anyone, even the Allies, to know what they were doing.

"Wait," Alphonse said, putting his hand up to stop the other Frenchmen from snapping the picture. Then he waved at Taffy, motioning him to join us in the picture and said we should have an Englishman, too so that all the Allies are together. After snapping his picture, he asked Taffy to join in the funeral to represent the British in the Honor Guard. Taffy seemed pleased with this honor. He then said, that he had come to retrieve his wire hanger and left.

"Does he know what is going on?" I asked.

"No, but he is welcome to help us with the funeral," he said smiling. "No one knows what is in the box after it is nailed shut."

I smiled back and said; "I'll see you tomorrow, then."

He paused, looking down the hall quickly, and the two of them went down the stairs.

From left to right: Alphonse de la Haye, Head of French Underground; Trevor Evans, English Paratrooper; and Sy Brenner, Head of Surgical Room.

This is the photograph taken in the Verbandzimmer on that day. Alphonse de la Haye, pictured here on the left, sent the picture to Sy Brenner after the war. Taffy is in the center, and Sy Brenner is on the right dressed in a white smock. At the time this picture was taken, Taffy was unaware that the purpose of the photograph was so that members of the French Underground would know what Brenner looked like. He was the man they could trust. Sy Brenner continued to work with the French Underground until the end of the war. Brenner was later told that the Germans were looking for de la Haye, and that the whole time, they were looking for him, he was there; hiding in their own P.O.W. infirmary.

The next morning, Taffy and I went downstairs and out the door. It was a brisk morning as we joined the procession standing near the gate. We watched as Taffy took his place next to the right wheel of the wagon that held the box. I took my place next to the left wheel, and then the French soldiers began to assemble behind us. About ten feet behind the cart was the Padre, followed by two guys who held up wooden poles that had large banners attached to them. Although I'm not sure what the other banner signified, at least one of them had the name St. Vincent emblazoned on it with what must have been some kind of religious symbolism. In any case, it all seemed very solemn and serious at the time. I suspect that had I been raised a Catholic, I might have understood what it was all about. The Padre walked right behind the cart. Behind the banners, the French soldiers formed into a column, four across, and must have totaled about thirty-five to forty guys. I saw the guy who was supposed to be in the box, standing in the middle, looking down at the ground. I wondered who he was and why it was so important to sneak him out of the camp.

After exiting the gates of the Lazarett, the procession turned left and went down the road in a direction I had never been before. We passed through some fields. There were railroad tracks to the right of the road. We walked about fifteen minutes until we came to an old German cemetery. The French had already dug a hole in the back of the cemetery. The box was removed from the wagon and the French Padre stood at foot of the box. Everyone looked very sad. Prayers were said. One of the other Frenchmen started talking. I assumed he was saying what a wonderful man the guy was. Some more prayers were said, all in French. Then, after removing the dog tags from the box, it was lowered into the ground.

Above: Funeral March

This is a picture of the funeral procession taken that day. Brenner is not in the picture. He was standing next to the casket in a place of honor. The French soldier whose dog tags were nailed to the box, is somewhere in the middle.

The Padre said a few more prayers. Then, a Frenchmen called out something else. We all stood at attention and saluted.

The tags were then nailed to a white cross that someone had made. The cross was pounded down into the ground above the grave as the dirt was shoveled back in. Before the hole was completely covered, the guards had us marching back to the camp.

It was nice to be outdoors for a while, walking through the fields, even under the watchful eyes of our German captors. I walked along next to Alphonse wondering about all that had happened today.

When I looked around, I didn't see the French soldier anywhere. He was already gone.

"Why was it so important that you get that particular man out of the camp today?" I asked, adding, "I'll understand if you can't tell me."

"Well, it is very simple, you see," he said quietly. "He is very good with explosives, and we have managed to acquire some recently. There really isn't anything that we want to blow up in the camp, so he must be outside."

He trudged along, gazing at the railroad tracks off to the left and said, "The trains go through here taking German soldiers to my country. As Man of Confidence, it is important that you understand why we want to stop those trains. I am glad you are willing to help us. It is good to be Allies, yes? Our friend knows how to blow up bridges and overpasses. He knows how to stop the trains."

When we parted at the door to the Verbandzimmer, he offered his hand in friendship, this time he covered the handshake with his left hand, his grip stronger, and I knew I had made an important friend.

*The war ended with the surrender of Japan in August
1945. While on the train home, I was getting antsy
with mixed emotions. It occurred to me that even
though my brother was in combat all the time overseas,
he still took time to write me, even after I was declared
missing. All of his letters were returned to my home.
I now realized how much he loved me.*

CHAPTER 20

The Lady

We had been talking that night, before drifting off to sleep, about how guys were disappearing in the middle of the night recently. It was normal for patients to come and go, but now, some of the medics were disappearing too.

One by one, each guy finally fell asleep, leaving me to be the last one awake. It was the same way each night, leaving us alone with our thoughts. I had more to think about than most. I had more to worry about then the others. I had more to fear.

First of all, being in charge of the Verbandzimmer, I was very concerned about Whitey's operation without having the proper equipment or even a decent place and having a qualified surgeon. Then, being the M.O.C., I was responsible for a lot of what was going on, and guys were relying on me to take care of things, but those were the little concerns. What really kept me awake was sleeping in the bed above me. Had Chris told anybody about me being a Jew?

These are the kinds of thoughts that started every night for me as I lay there shivering on those dark frozen nights. The same worries. I had the same memories of my family back home as a way to calm my fears every night. It was the same pattern of thoughts to go from anxiety, to calm, to finally sleep.

It was on this night I found out how men disappeared at night and then they were shipped out.

I was in a deep sleep when I felt a hand cupped firmly over my mouth and another mouth actually touching my ear whispering, "Don't make a sound, no harm will come to you, just very quietly come with us."

Staring up, I could see that it was the guard, "Johnny," and I was at first relieved until I saw who was with him. It was Little Caesar. Shit. If he was here in the middle of the night, this couldn't be good.

Sitting on the side of the bunk to put my boots on, I could feel Caesar's firm grip on my upper arm as he handed me my jacket. They motioned for me to come with them down the stairs and Johnny told me to walk between them; both of the guards had rifles slung over their shoulders. I thought they were going to shoot me, and why not? They marched me out the front door and down a path in the snow, past the guards at the gate, and turned right at the end of the barbed wire enclosure. This meant that we were going away from the Stalag.

I was shivering from the cold and shaking from fear. The moon shined brightly on the windblown snow. Thoughts were running through my mind. Did Chris turn me in? Was this "Beshert"? Was this the way I was going to die? Will my poor mother ever know whatever became of me? I couldn't figure it out.

What made me even more uncomfortable was that Little Caesar had his hand on my arm as though he was guiding me, and then, after a certain part of the way, he shoved me ahead of the two of them. As soon as that happened, I was sure my time was up and they were going to shoot me, so I started praying, "Shema Yisrael, Adonai Eloheynu, Adonai Ehad," over and over again.

Then, Johnny stopped me and started talking. He said, "We will soon come to a house; you will knock on the door. A lady will answer. She will invite you in, and you will not give her your name. She will not give you hers; just call her, "The Lady."

Then he gave me a little shove and said, "OK, keep going toward the house."

I walked across the field toward the house, but my mind was racing. I was trying to figure out what the hell was going on.

"Go on, go on!" Johnny urged, "And hurry up about it."

I slowly began to walk across the field. Was this a trick so that they could shoot me in the back? I kept looking back at them to see if they were pointing their rifles at me. Soon I reached the house and looked back once more. The two guards were standing there gesturing to me to just knock on the door.

I knocked on the door and a woman opened it. She said, "I am The Lady, please come in." The first thing that I noticed was a large portrait of an SS general above the fireplace. Then, I thought I'd really had it.

She saw the look on my face and said, "Don't pay any attention to that son of a bitch. He's my husband, but I didn't know what he was when I married him." She told me that she was brought up in Heidelberg, and that her father was a professor at the university there.

From the outside, the house looked like most of the houses in the area, but it was a little removed from the rest of the town, surrounded by fields as it was. It was very clean and well kept up. I was impressed with the furnishings, which seemed almost out of place considering the rural surroundings. I guess generals do pretty well.

I figured The Lady must have been in her late thirties, but at my age, in my condition, who could tell? She was an attractive blond, typically Germanic looking, with her hair combed straight back in a bun like my mother's was. She wore a cameo pin on a print dress with a white collar. I followed her movements and noticed she had a very nice figure, but wore no hose and wore shoes that looked like they were men's shoes.

She told me to follow her down to the cellar where I saw a couch, a table, and some chairs. Against the far wall was a radio that looked like it had a sending set. On the wall above the radio was a large clock.

She said, "We have a little more than twelve minutes, so I will explain some things to you. I will only be known to you as, "The Lady," and you will only be known as, "Kokomo" and you will only reveal what you learn here to someone who tells you he comes from 'Shamokin'. In all probability, Shamokin will be a different person each time you are contacted."

She then turned on the radio. In a few minutes, through the static, we heard the news on the BBC from London. Some of the news was very disturbing. It was about our losses at the Battle of the Bulge.

When the news was concluded, they said, "Stand by for some important announcements."

The announcements were all coded messages like:

"Mary had a little lamb her fleece was as green as grass but at times her fleece is as white as snow," or, "Joe's wife had twins." Another one I remember was simply, "Jack and Jill went down the hill."

We sat and listened to these messages, which were meaningless, at least they were to me, for about twenty-five to thirty minutes. Occasionally, she would look at the clock and write a note down on a pad she kept on the table next to the radio.

Suddenly, she grabbed my arm and said, "Wait, this one is for you!"

"The circus is coming to town."

All this waiting for that short message. I didn't know what it meant.

"What does it mean?" I asked The Lady.

"I don't know, and you don't want to know," she answered. "You can't tell what you don't know."

I followed her up the stairs, my eyes glued on her beautiful figure. All this time, I was sitting here scared, and I wasn't thinking about the fact that she was such a beautiful woman. Boy, I really had been cooped up too long.

"It's time for you to go," she said as we reached the top of the stairs. I think she must have been reading my thoughts. Damn.

As she saw me to the door, she reminded me, "Remember, don't tell anyone anything about this meeting or about me. Someone will give you the code word 'Shamokin' and you are to give them the message. Then just forget it. Do you understand?"

"Yes, I do," I answered.

I wrapped my thin field jacket tightly around me against the wind as I went down the steps to the path away from the house. Off in the distance, I could see Johnny and Little Caesar standing under some trees, hands stuffed in their pockets for warmth. As I got closer to them, I could see that they both had large grins, even smiles on their faces. Little Caesar, of all people, had a smile on his face. That was the first and last time I had seen him smile. His teeth were very white against his dark olive skin. He really had us fooled. It looks like this whole thing was "Beshert".

In the last of my four nightmares, I turn my gaze from the window of the Verbandzimmer only to catch sight of some grizzly, ghastly object sticking out over the edge of a large bucket. I focus on it and see it is a severed human leg, cut off above the knee, with a few inches of bone extending out from the bloody, purulent flesh.

CHAPTER 21

Whitey

Johnny and Caesar were kidding around with each other as we walked back to the Lazarett. The atmosphere walking back from The Lady's house was quite different from what it was when we had left the Lazarett earlier in the evening. When we left the Lazarett, I had been terrified that I was on my way to my own execution. Now I felt, if not like a free man, at least like a man with hope. It was meant to be. It was "Beshert".

So much had happened in such a short time that I was also a little bit confused. I needed time to process what was happening to me. I was having a hard time believing what I had just experienced. I was sure no one else would ever believe that it had happened.

If I ever did get home and tried to tell my brother Myer, he would just laugh at my incredible imagination. "Ah, you're full of shit. If you are going to tell a story, at least tell one that is believable."

My brother Myer was always teasing me when I was growing up. Once, when I was about five years old, I was playing in the vacant lot next to our house and got chased home by five of the kids who lived in the four-plex on the other side of the lot. My brother said they were, "hillbillies," but I didn't know what that meant. They were all around my age, but there were five of them, and one of me, so I ran home. When I got to our house, Myer was standing on the porch. He decided to have some fun with them at my expense.

"Now it isn't fair for you to fight with him all at once. You can all vote and decide which one of you wants to fight him first, and the others need to stand back on the other side of the lot and wait their turn," said Myer with a very stern look on his face.

While they decided who was going to fight me first, I looked at him like he was crazy. "Listen up," he said to me in a quiet voice, "They are going to send the biggest kid, and he's going to be a lot bigger then you. I'm going to point up in the air and yell, 'Look at the airplane stuck in the mud!' and when he looks up to see the airplane, that's when you hit him as hard as you can, right in the kisser. Then, you run back up the stairs and back into the house as fast as you can." Myer was always having fun like this at my expense.

All the way back to the camp, Johnny and Caesar were jabbering to each other, not saying much to me at all. I couldn't figure out why I was picked to do this. Did they pick me because I was the M.O.C.? Was it because of my connection with Alphonse? Did The Lady know about Alphonse, or did they work separately? I'd better be careful not to tell her about him or him about her.

As we neared the gate, I was placed between Johnny and Caesar again, and I noticed that Caesar had gotten his usual scowl back. Now, I understood what his scowl was all about. Being as mean as he was to the prisoners, he was the last person anyone would suspect of helping us.

When we went in the building, Johnny said, "You better get some sleep. I'll be coming to wake everyone up soon. You don't want anyone to know you were gone last night."

I took off my boots before going up the stairs so as not to make any noise. It was about 3:00 or 4:00 a.m. and I should have been tired but I felt wide-awake.

I didn't feel so wide-awake when Johnny woke everyone up just a few hours later. It didn't help to know that he didn't get any more sleep than I did. I got up and tried my best to act as if nothing had happened the night before.

When I arrived in the Verbandzimmer, the French soldier who had been there with Alphonse before was there for a dressing change. He seemed quite proud of the fact that he spoke English, which he actually did quite well. He told me that Alphonse was a wanted man by the Germans. He had a price on his head. The Germans wanted him, and they didn't know that they already had him, hiding right under their noses, in plain sight.

After he had gone, I started to inventory my supplies, and I was upset to see several rolls of toilet paper unraveled on the side table. The wet dressings were causing me to use a lot more toilet paper, and it was getting harder and harder to come by. It upset me that someone was so careless with my supplies. As I started to roll it back up, I felt something very cold and hard underneath the pile of paper. I was startled to find a Beretta handgun. At first, I thought it might be Paddy's, but then I realized that the Frenchmen must have left it and that if so, he must have left it for me.

I quickly checked to see if it was loaded. It was, I made sure the safety was on. I put it in my pocket, glancing toward the door to make sure no one had seen.

I don't know how long I was standing there staring at the door. I didn't know what to do or what to think. Things were getting more and more complicated and more and more dangerous.

Did The Lady know about the French? Did they know about her? Did anyone know I was a Jew? Had Chris said anything to anyone? How was I going to get everything I needed for Whitey's operation?

I knew I had better start working on that right away. I went out into the hall and found Henk Das.

"Henk, I'm going to need to talk to the Commandant about getting more medical supplies. Can you set it up?" I asked.

Henk shook his head in the affirmative, tapped his brow with his forefinger and went off down the stairs.

It was just as well; I hadn't been harassing the Commandant as much as I should be. After all, that was my job as M.O.C.. At least now when I started in on the Commandant, I would have some legitimate reasons. The Commandant was no fool. He could tell if I was complaining just to complain.

The guys started to bring patients to the Verbandzimmer, and I told them to bring Whitey right away because I didn't know when I was going to the Commandant, and I wanted to make sure he got taken care of. When they brought him in, he had his usual smile on his face, but I could tell that he was uncomfortable and probably scared.

"How you doing, Doc?" Whitey asked good-naturedly. He always seemed to want to put me at ease, as if I was the patient and not the other way around.

"I'm doing great, Whitey. I got a new song for you." And then, I would sing some silly, made up song like, "Sweet Eloise has a Venereal Disease."

He'd laugh dutifully and always say, "You always got a new one for me, don't you Doc?"

"I stay up nights composing them for you."

We would have this same type of banter almost every time he came in, even though each time he came in he looked, worse than the time before. We'd talk as I'd unwrap his old dressing, clean out the area around the bone which remained exposed, and then repack the area.

Whitey must have sensed that there was something different today. "What's up, Doc? You look like you want to tell me something that you don't want to tell me, if you know what I mean."

"Yeah, I do Whitey," I said. I stopped working on his dressing and looked him in the eyes. It would have been easier to look at the dressing and keep on working on his wounds while I talked, but I respected him too much for that. The wound was more discolored and pussy today than it had been the day before.

"Your leg's getting worse Whitey. You know that, don't you?"

He shook his head in agreement, staring me in the eye but not saying a word.

"You want to live don't you?" I asked. "If you want to live, were going to have to take the leg."

I looked at him hard, wanting to be sure he understood. Sometimes when you tell a guy something hard like this, they just find a way to misunderstand. Whitey wasn't like that. I'm sure he knew this was coming all along.

"I want to live, Doc." He said. "I understand what you're telling me. It's OK."

It was as if he was trying to make it easier for me again. That was the way Whitey was.

"You were meant to live Whitey, that's why you made it this far. Right?" I asked in a positive voice.

"Right, Doc," he answered.

"Now don't worry about the operation. I found a first-class surgeon to do it." I told him, squeezing his hand. "I'll be with you all the way, too".

Squeezing his hand, I realized how weak Whitey had become. His wound wasn't the only problem. He was all skin and bone. No muscle. No meat on his body. Just a skeleton covered with skin.

It wasn't just Whitey that looked like a skeleton. We were all starting to look like that. Maybe, if Whitey had better nutrition, his wound would have healed better. Maybe, losing his leg wouldn't have necessary.

A couple hours later, a GI came in to have a dressing change on his shoulder.

As I started to remove the old dressing, he smiled at me and said, "I'm from Shamokin. Where are you from?"

"Kokomo," I answered. I didn't know his name, and he didn't know mine. That's the way it was meant to be: "Beshert".

I gave him the message, and I presume he took it back to the camp and passed it on as he was supposed to do. This was the first of many such meetings; just as The Lady had said, it was a different guy from "Shamokin" every time. From now on, I became very suspicious of everyone, having heard that the men in the general population of the Stalag had discovered several German plants. It seemed that the Krauts were good at infiltrating spies into our ranks-usually men who had once lived in the good old U.S.A.. Canny P.O.W.'s would catch them mostly on questions about baseball and popular songs.

I was visiting The Lady about three times a week, and now, and no one appeared to know about it. Little Caesar did a great job keeping up his cover by acting mean as hell. A few weeks later, he took me part of the way to The Lady's, and met me at a designated spot when I was done. I suspected that he and Johnny had a couple of gals to keep them company while I was on my mission. I always returned just before dawn, and a few times, I slept a couple of hours in one of The Lady's bedrooms, on a comfortable feather bed. On one such visit, she introduced me to her two daughters. Beautiful, and very tempting! But, it was The Lady herself who really turned me on. I was too scared, and too much in awe of her ever to try anything, but oh, how I dreamed about her. I loved to watch from below as she walked up the stairs; I could see her underwear through her sheer dress, and that always produced a highly characteristic physical reaction in me, if you know what I mean! On this night, at the height of my sexy fantasies, I could hear outside, in the distance, a troop of German soldiers marching by in their hobnail boots-a truly eerie experience that brought me right back to reality.

That night, I heard hobnail boots of two combat soldiers coming down the hall. They asked Bruno where the Vertrannsman (Man of Confidence) was. Bruno said, "Brenner," and pointed to my room. They ordered me to follow them, and they took me down to the main floor and across a dim hall, all the way to the end. Sticking out of a doorway, I saw the rear end of the prison's diminutive French Priest. One of the soldiers grabbed the Priest by the collar and hurled him in the air all the way across the hallway and against the wall; the impact knocked the poor padre unconscious. Inside the room, which was no bigger than a walk-in closet, I observed a corpse on a stretcher against the wall. The body was stitched from below the navel all the way up to the breastbone. I was impressed with how well done it was. It was done by a doctor. The space beside the stretcher and the wall left only enough room to stand in. They motioned for me to remove the dog tags, and as I squatted beside the stretcher, the two soldiers started laughing behind me and slammed the door shut. There I was for three days and nights in a closet with no windows or light and only enough room to stand or squat. I vomited most of the time I was in there. The stench from the corpse was getting worse, as well as the vomit. Throughout this hideous experience, I was quite sure I was going to die. The only way I could breathe was by sucking air through the small space between the bottom of the door and the floor. Imagine doing that for three days and nights on end! Every four or five minutes, I yelled for help. Finally, the guard we called Johnny heard me and let me out. He told me he had been looking all over for me because this was going to be a very cold night. That was the signal that I was going to see The Lady. He took me to the guard's room, where I was cleaned up, he gave me a new shirt, and pants, but I had no underwear.

I was still sick from malnutrition, diarrhea and ulcerative colitis. At the age of twenty-three, I was supposed to be at the prime of my life, but like many others who went to war, many of us felt like lost souls, even though we were happy to get out of the service. I have had a lot of time to think and spend a lot of sleepless nights, having nightmares and reliving my sleepless nights in Stalag V-A. The nights were long and dark.

CHAPTER 22

Hitler's Little Bastards

From the window in the Verbandzimmer, I could see the castle in the center of Ludwigsberg. I had never seen a castle before, and the story I had heard about this one intrigued me. It was King Ludwig's castle, and the town was named after him. I had heard somewhere that the castle was famous for having one of the most beautiful courtyards and gardens in Europe. I could also see the Krankenhaus, just to the right of the castle. Whenever I looked out the window, I would fantasize about being able to see the inside of the castle. It was said that it was from in that castle that the Grimm Brothers had written the fairy tale of Rapunzel.

The morning after I had spoken to the Commandant about getting supplies, I was looking out that window at the castle and the Krankenhaus when I heard hobnailed boots coming up the stairs. I always got a little nervous when I heard that sound. Our guards didn't wear hobnailed boots. They were worn by German combat troops, and it was very seldom that they came into the Lazarett. When they did come, it usually meant trouble.

I anxiously looked toward the door as the sound reached the top of the stairs, just in time to see Henk Das enter the room with a German soldier I had never seen before.

"This guy is from the Krankenhaus. The Commandant arranged for him to escort you there to get the supplies you requested." Henk looked impressed that the Commandant had acted so swiftly. I was totally surprised myself. Henk handed me a piece of paper with German writing on it, a stamp that said, "Kriegegef Lazarett Stalag V-A." It looked like an order form of some kind but, I didn't know what. What I did notice was that it had the wrong date on it. The date read 8 December 1944. So much had happened in such a short amount of time that I was rarely sure of the date. But, I knew that we had already celebrated Christmas, so I knew the date was off. I mentioned this to Henk, and he said not to worry about it. He said to give the paper to the supply person at the Krankenhaus, and they would give me the supplies I needed.

As we walked out the door, I put on an old French Army hat I had found, and a World War I Polish officer's coat I had traded some cigarettes for. It was made of flimsy felt and was powder blue but I figured the added layer would keep me warmer. I had my GI jacket underneath it, but it wasn't enough for this kind of cold weather.

Left: The form given to Sy Brenner to take to the Krankenhaus to obtain supplies.

The guard didn't say anything as we walked along. Occasionally, the people from the town would stare at me, but they didn't say anything until we reached a corner near the castle. There were some kids who looked like they were about eleven or twelve years old and were wearing Hitler Youth uniforms. At first, they couldn't tell where I was from because of my mixed up clothing. I was kind of glad about that, but the guard ruined things by telling them I was an American. Then, they really gave it to me, increasing their insults, now in English. One of the boys spoke perfect English. He said he was being trained to be the Burgermeister of a small town in England when they take it, and if it weren't for the Americans entering the war, they would be in England already. He said he was very lucky because his friend was being trained to be a Burgermeister in a town close to the one he'd be placed. Then he hit me with a bolt that I didn't expect. That little bastard told me that they were going to eliminate all the Jews in England. These were the little guys who would turn their parents in for the slightest remark that didn't suit them. I couldn't imagine what this kid would grow up to be. The thought was chilling.

I asked them where they got their uniforms. They said they were from the Hitler Youth Program. They were being trained to seek out and kill all enemies of the Third Reich. They said that when they were done conquering England, the United States was next.

When I asked how they were going to do that, they said that they have already started to take over the country.

"I have an uncle who is the Commandant of the Nazi Bund in New York City. There are bunds all over the United States." The little bastard was right. I remembered seeing newsreels about them before the war.

After listening to that sickening child, I was boiling inside and did everything I could to keep my composure and not swat him. Thinking about the position I was in, I asked him if he missed his mother while he was away in camp.

"We don't think of things like that." He said, "We are learning to keep a clear head and winning the war." He smiled up at me puffing out his chest boastfully, "We are the greatest nation in the world and the Fuehrer is the greatest leader."

His friend didn't say anything, but nodded his approval as the guard nudged me on my way, and we left those brats standing there on the corner.

I was more than a little worried as we continued on our way to the Krankenhaus. Back home, the newsreels in the theaters had been full of demonstrations of Nazi Bund meetings all over America. It seemed like thousands of people were there sieg heiling, shouting, "Heil Hitler." We would also read every so often about the 5th columnist; spies who had been arrested by the FBI. Hollywood had made a lot of movies about spies.

The Krankenhaus

When I got to the Krankenhaus, I was shown downstairs to the pharmacy, in the basement. I handed the attendant the paper the Commandant had provided me with and started to tell him what I needed--sterile gauze and bandages mostly, but other things, too.

"Nein, nein, nein," was all I heard. The guy on the other side of the counter started piling up a supply of toilet paper and bottles of kalen and some rolls of cotton batten. The same old stuff; I was bluntly told that they didn't have what I needed, but they would send my usual supplies tomorrow, as it was too much for me to carry.

Exasperated, I looked around me and noticed the French doctor who had also played at our Christmas party. He stood, arms folded, leaning against the door, shaking his head from side to side with a grim smile on his face. I could see from the look in his eyes that I would never see the supplies that I really needed. I guess it was "Beshert". I had hoped that I could get the guard to walk back to the Lazarett by way of the castle and gardens so I could see them, but that wasn't meant to be either.

I passed Johnny in the hall on my way back to the Verbandzimmer. "It looks like it's going to be another cold night." He said with a wink. (That was our signal that it was time to go see The Lady).

The nights in prison camp actually became precious to me as I filled up the hours with the realization-played over and over again in my mind-of what a wonderful family I had. I remember looking up and catching a glimpse of my father smiling as he puffed on his pipe. I caught my mother's eye, while she was smiling with a look of love and approval. My mother would wipe a tear from her eye.

It took this wretched prison experience to make me realize all that I had.

CHAPTER 23

Surgery

Dr. Wroznotofski showed up at 6:30 on the morning of Whitey's surgery. Two German soldiers carrying his supplies accompanied him. I wasn't sure if they were medics or guards from the hospital, but he treated them as if they were his assistants.

I was just getting out of bed myself and didn't expect him so early. The day before, as he had instructed, I had a cleaning crew in to wash down the small room he wanted to use. Everything was washed, the ceiling, the walls, the window, the floor. The table in the center of the room was scrubbed and a small table was brought in and put next to the window, and it was scrubbed down as well. Since he said he was bringing his own instruments, thank God for that. I figured we were as ready as we were going to be.

By the time I got down the hall, he had already told Henk that he wanted the room cleaned again. He seemed to want them to put special attention on cleaning the window. No matter how much they scrubbed the inside of that window, there was no way we could clean the outside of it and no way could we get more light into the room. It didn't seem light enough to me to do something like this, but the Doc kept giving instructions through Henk Das on what else needed cleaning. He was all business and I was glad to have him.

He brought with him three sheets, a couple of basins, some large bowls, a jar of a rather strong smelling liquid soap, and his surgical instruments wrapped up in two towels. He also had a small can of ether that we would use to put Whitey to sleep. I was glad he wouldn't have to bite down on the bite stick to ease the pain.

Once the table was cleaned a second time, a clean sheet was placed on it and rolled up on one end to be used for Whitey's head. The other supplies were put on the small table, and we were ready to begin.

Henk and I watched Dr. Wroznotofski arranging his things on the table the way he wanted them. Henk told me that the Commandant was also sending us a second physician to help. I was glad to hear that he was an English Doctor, a Major Gordon.

"He was a member of the Red Berets that jumped at Arnhem," explained Henk. "He should be here any minute."

This made me feel a little better; at least Major Gordon spoke English.

Just then, the door opened and Gordon walked in with a snappy, "Well then, are we ready to proceed?"

Dr. Wroznotofski took one look at him and started yelling and screaming, but I didn't have a clue what it was that touched him off. All I saw was that he was physically pushing Gordon out of the room. I looked at Henk in alarm.

"He is upset, saying that this man is no kind of surgeon, walking into a surgery with dirty fingernails and clothes."

I nervously looked at my own fingernails, which were thankfully clipped down to the nub. I was sorry to lose Major Gordon, I needed him for self-assurance, if nothing else, but there was nothing I could do about it now.

Whitey was brought in and placed on the table, stripped from the waist down, wearing a white t-shirt and a scared look on his face. I had performed some amputations in the field, removing a few dangling arms and legs, but nothing at all like this. Now, I found myself tormented by horrific flashbacks of guys on the battlefield yelling and screaming, "Don't cut off my fucking leg!"

I was thankful for the ether; I don't know if I could stand hearing Whitey scream as we took his leg. I had heard too many men screaming, worrying about losing their legs, and I didn't want to hear a great kid like Whitey scream when he was losing his.

Following the doctor's instructions, I started scrubbing Whitey's leg with the liquid soap from above the point where the bone was exposed and the skin started up to his groin. The whole time I was doing this, Whitey just stared up at the ceiling.

The doctor had sent his two Krauts downstairs with the large bowls to fill them with hot water. We didn't have any hot water upstairs. Then Wroznotofski and I both started washing our hands, using the first bowl.

Henk translated the doctor's instructions about how I was to administer the either by holding a two-inch wad of gauze over Whitey's face and dripping some of the ether into the wad. I started doing this as Dr. Wroznotofski started poking around the wound. I guess he was trying to decide how high up he was going to have to cut it. It didn't take long for Whitey to pass out.

The doc asked Henk how I was doing, and I told him. "Whitey's out and this ether is starting to get to me. We better hurry and get this done."

I was worried I would pass out, too and ruin the whole thing. I was told to wash my hands again and Henk took over with the ether. Wroznotofski started cutting the skin much farther up from the point where I thought we were going to have to take his leg. He was in such a foul mood, I was afraid to ask him about it. I looked at Henk, and he just shrugged his shoulders, his head turned slightly away, trying to avoid the fumes.

As the doctor cut away skin and tissue, he had me scoop the litter off the table into a basin to keep the area as clean as possible. Then, he had me lift the leg up so he could cut away some of the skin and tissue from the backside of the leg as well, but this was cut lower down. I was concerned that he wasn't cutting evenly, that maybe he didn't really know what he was doing after all.

Had I let Whitey down?

"Doc, Doc," Henk's voice pulled me out of my brief episode of self-doubt, explaining that the doctor wanted me to stand next to Whitey's upper body and pull back the skin from the leg.

Doing this exposed the bone more and more, but Wroznotofski wasn't satisfied.

"He says you have to pull harder," explained Henk, "He can't see the bone enough."

It seemed to be taking a long time. I was pulling as hard as I could and the Doctor was snipping a little, pulling a little. I couldn't really see what he was doing, so as I pulled I rested my head on my arms as I felt myself getting very tired. I couldn't understand why I was so groggy. It was still early in the day.

I guess I wasn't really paying attention, because I felt the saw before I saw it. I felt something wet hit me in the cheek near my eye, and I jerked my head out of the way and saw Wroznotofski sawing away at Whitey's leg. Watching him saw reminded me of my brother-in-law, Max, cutting a board to fix someone's roof with. Dr. Wroznotofski looked angry as he sawed. Bits of blood and bone splintered away from the saw, into the air. I couldn't take my eyes away, and he kept on sawing away until I could feel the vibration change, and I knew he was through.

He just picked up the leg and tossed it into a bucket under the table, the knee and bone sticking out over the top of the bucket, ugly and dripping. This grotesque image has remained with me ever since, and still comes to me in the form of a nightmare several times a week.

I was still pulling back on the skin and the doctor was busy doing something down there. I didn't want to look. I was glad I had a simple job to do so I didn't have to look. I just put my head back down on my forearm, wanting to weep.

Soon, Henk told me he wanted me to release the skin but to hold the leg up so that he could sew the flap. It actually came together rather nicely, like a final piece of a jigsaw puzzle.

Wroznotofski covered the sutures with a piece of gauze and started barking instructions to Henk as he washed his hands and started wrapping his instruments into a towel.

"He wants you to wrap it tightly with the gauze and to keep the dressing as tight as possible for the next twenty-four hours." Translating, Henk looked to the doctor to see if there was anything else. Wroznotofski walked out of the room, an angry look on his face, waving his hands like he wanted to wash his hands of the whole thing.

When I finished dressing the wound, I could see there wouldn't be enough to do it again the next day. I would have to use toilet paper.

I quickly finished wrapping the stump and pushed my way out the door into the hall as a cleanup crew was coming in. I needed to get into the fresh air. I was sick to my stomach. I was confused. I was so mixed up, I walked right into a wall. I wanted to lay my head on a pillow. Somehow, I remembered pillows. I had one at home.

I stumbled down the hall to the Verbandzimmer. Closing the door, I sat on the table breathing deeply, trying not to think. I didn't want to see anyone.

The bandage room was much brighter and better ventilated than where we had done the operation. I started to feel a little better, especially after some of the men came by and congratulated me, as if I'd saved Whitey's life all by myself. For the rest of the day, I just sat on the table, looking out the window at the castle, thinking about my pillow at home.

Much to my pleasure, for the rest of the time I was in that wretched prison camp, Whitey visited me at least once a week. He always came in hopping all over the place on his one leg, kidding around, repeating my bad old jokes and songs, and thanking me over and over again. Even today, I wonder what became of him and how he is doing.

*Early in April, a man we knew only as, "The Colonel"
said, "There should be a Sam Brenner in every prison
camp, in charge of morale."
That might have been the greatest compliment anyone
ever gave me!*

CHAPTER 24

Liberation Approaches: "The Colonel"

The Australian colonel was a mysterious character, who, while seldom seen, was a great presence in our lives nevertheless. I can only relate a little bit about him from actual experience; others in my immediate circle told me most of what I know about him. I never actually learned his name; everyone just called him, "The Colonel." One thing about him seemed certain-he was on the Germans' hit list.

All I knew about him was that he was in the Lazarett when I got there. He wasn't a patient, though. One of the medics told me he was in the Lazarett for the second time, and that he gave the Germans a giant pain in the ass.

According to the legend of the camp, The Colonel had been taken prisoner in Africa, whereupon he immediately assumed command of all British and British Commonwealth prisoners. He organized them into committees for escapes, sabotage, and obtaining help from the outside. Neither could the Germans control him, nor could they kill him, as they soon found out, because he made sure that the Red Cross inspectors knew of him. On one of the rare Red Cross tours of a camp in which The Colonel was incarcerated, he stepped out and demanded better food and more humane conditions. He told the inspectors that what lay before their eyes was a sham, and all would be reversed as soon as they left. A German guard stepped forward to slam him with a rifle butt, which turned out to be a good break for The Colonel. The Red Cross inspector told the Commandant in no uncertain terms that it was apparent the camp administration wasn't living up to the Geneva. Convention, and that the Red Cross fully expected that the Commandant do so. Moreover, the Red Cross would require a daily report from the administration as to The Colonel's whereabouts and well-being.

The Germans wanted this man eliminated, but it would have to be done in a legal way. They found the best way to control him was to incarcerate him in prison hospitals. There he couldn't mingle with the general kriegie population and incite the prisoners or plan escapes for wounded or sick men or for medics, who on fear of court-martial weren't allowed to escape. In order to get rid of The Colonel, the Germans contrived to take him for a ride, so to speak. They'd ship him from one Stalag to another by boxcar, which were often strafed by Allied fighter planes. Almost all German boxcars were well, "air-conditioned" with .50 caliber machine gun bullet holes. Now, on what was reputed to be his third trip to our camp, we felt that the war was about to end and, that it would be a shame to let that man suffer another ride in a boxcar. The Allies had complete control of the air by this time, and it was a sure bet that they would finish The Colonel off. Tall, gaunt and very frail, he looked much older than his years.

The Aussies in the Lazarett finally devised a scheme that would create an illusion. The Lazarett had a third floor. The Krauts used the main floor, and the medics and patients used the second floor, but the third was never used except for the Christmas party. The Aussies figured out a way to hide The Colonel on the third floor and make it appear that he had escaped. One of them found a crawl hole in the ceiling that no one had ever noticed before. They investigated and decided here was the best place, in spite of the fact that it was difficult getting him up and then down when he needed to be down. Several of the men each donated a slat from their bunks to wall off a solid area with 2x4s above the ceiling, and with a little hay from each man's bunk, they made a mattress. Each of us took turns sharing our rations, and there was always someone to guard the stair to the third floor. The lookout would use hand signals to notify the rest of us if any German guard came into the area. We brought The Colonel down to our floor when he had to use the latrine or if he wanted to chat a little.

My job in this affair was to bring The Colonel down when he needed to use the latrine or happened to be desperate for a little human contact. These were always hair-raising moments, although we did sometimes have pleasant conversations. One time, he asked me what I had done before the war. I told him I was going to school, and that I was a radio actor. "Someday this war's going to end. You know that, don't you Sam? And then you'll go back to school," he replied.

His words stopped me right in my tracks. Thoughts of home flooded into my mind. I wondered what my parents were doing right then, and if my brother Myer, was even still alive.

"What about you, Colonel," I asked. "Where do you come from?" "Brisbane," he said. "My wife's holding down our little plot of ground while I'm off conquering the world."

Bruno's signal from the stairs interrupted my laughter. I sprang up and led The Colonel back to his stairway. He'd barely gotten to the top of the stairs when the sound of hobnailed boots rang out from the bandage room.

We watched with glee as the guards ravaged the Lazarett in search of their quarry, and we secretly laughed as they threw all the hay-filled mattresses off each bunk not even realizing that the slats were missing. They were puzzled: how can a man escape from a compound within a compound? No one had ever escaped from a Lazarett before. The Commandant was boiling mad; the scam had proven a great success. The Aussies were beside themselves with joy, certain that their Colonel had gotten away safely. For my part, I worried that this escapade would bring down more scrutiny on the rest of us, especially considering the other risky games we were playing at the moment-Alphonse and the phony funerals; Johnny, Little Caesar and me taking our night walks, for example. Even so, I felt as if I had dealt just one more blow to the Nazis, and was therefore one more step closer to getting the hell out of there and going home to Detroit.

The Dog Fight

Some time in April, for a period of about two weeks, Paddy Green and I actually had a bit of fun together gazing out the second-floor window of the Verbandzimmer at some hair-raising events going on not too far away. From there, we had a clear view of a major railroad line two or three miles in the distance. We could see a tiny station that had only an overhanging sign to mark it, like a trolley stop. It said Ludwigsburg. Every day at around four o'clock, four P-47 dive bombers would come in and attack the little station. Then, the Germans would send out a detail of prisoners to clean it up. It appeared to us as if the Americans were egging on the Luftwaffe to come out and fight. One day, after two weeks of this taunting, the P-47s roared in right on schedule, but this time six Messerschmitts came out of nowhere in hot pursuit. As soon as the P-47 pilots noticed them, the American planes executed a precision loop into the sun. The next thing we saw astounded us-six US P-38 fighter planes emerged seemingly right out of the sun and shot down all six German planes.

It was the first time I had seen a P-38, a twin-fuselage plane that was the fastest we had before the advent of jets. Paddy and I jumped up and down like kids. It was like watching a movie, and we couldn't wait to spread the news. It made for a happy day in Stalag V-A.

Passover

Although, for most inmates of a P.O.W. camp, the passage of time seems hard to calculate, I always knew that the arrival of April would mean Easter. Much more important to me, however, was the Jewish holiday Passover, which always occurred a few days before. Inevitably, this generated thoughts of my family and the sweet time we had together at our Seders-the ritual Passover meals. I didn't dare attempt to celebrate the occasion this year, though, because it remained vital to conceal my Jewish identity as well as I could. One prayer uttered out loud, I thought, and I'd be done for.

A British paratroop officer with a long, twirled handlebar mustache across his face, Captain Rutherford, came into the camp to hold an Easter service. Some of the American and Brit prisoners decided to attend the service, and I thought I might go, too, if doing so helped to keep up appearances and otherwise avoid suspicion. The service made me good and homesick for Passover. If Chris was going to rat me out, that might have been the perfect occasion. Throughout the service, I kept looking around at the men, wondering if he had told any of them. This only made the experience more frightening.

The service included a recitation of the 23rd Psalm. Since this is a popular and much cherished text from the Hebrew Bible (Old Testament), I knew the words too, and joined in. All the while, I felt as if someone was watching me, which turned out to be true-John Alberti's eyes were boring right into me, although I couldn't figure out why he was so interested since he didn't know I was Jewish. Then it came to me; I was reciting the prayer by heart while most of the others in the assembly were reading it off a slip of paper. Alberti, son of a Lutheran minister, wasn't exactly a Bible-thumper, but he was probably pretty pious. Or, I suppose, it was possible that he didn't realize the Jewish origin of the Psalm. So for the time being, I contented myself with the thought he might be impressed by my own show of piety.

I have to admit that I felt pretty hypocritical standing there praying among Christians on Easter, even if I was reciting the 23rd Psalm. But from that day forward, John Alberti seemed to have become by greatest admirer. He had always hung around the Verbandzimmer, carrying litters in and out, and quiet as he was, no one paid much attention to him. Now, though, he followed me everywhere, chatting me up about every subject imaginable. He'd bring patients in on a litter and start talking. He stopped by between tasks, just to talk. When I went out to eat something, there he was right next to me, eating, too. It actually got to be more than a little annoying.

Even as a Jew among Gentiles, I appreciated the spiritual significance of the Easter service, and enjoyed the sense of solace and comradeship that came with the special gathering of the prisoners. I wondered, if under the circumstances, my parents would have been proud of me. Passover had always been a special time for our family. We celebrated as I imagined most Jewish families did: By cooking special dishes, reading in The Hagadah (the special Passover prayer book and guide to the Seder service) the story of how Moses rescued the Jews from bondage in Egypt, and going to the synagogue. When we came home from services, we would listen to my father read stories about the holiday.

On top of that, my family made its own special Passover observances-cleaning the house (and especially the kitchen) from top to bottom, laying out the clean white linens, large plates and colorful Austrian crystal that we used only for this holiday. According to tradition, we had to get rid of all the non-Kosher-for-Passover food in the house and replace it with that which had been specially blessed for the occasion. My own jobs each year at Passover-time included covering the wooden table and chairs in our kitchen with a fresh coat of white paint. All in all, it was a most special time.

Life in the camp had begun to change noticeably by April 1945. There weren't as many guards around, and the ones who were left weren't as alert as they had been before.

CHAPTER 25

Goodbye to The Lady

Nasty, old, "Little Caesar," the guard who had always accompanied Johnny and me on my trips to The Lady, was gone. Now, Johnny's face was drawn and haggard; he seemed to be walking in a stupor. On one of our last trips to The Lady's house, sometime around the first of May, he started talking about England and how nice it would be to see his family. His pace got slower the farther we walked. He told me that any day now the French or Americans would come and that we would all be liberated. He looked so distraught that I asked him if he wanted me to carry his rifle. He smiled at this and said it might not be a good idea because the German civilians were getting antsy.

When I arrived at The Lady's, she allowed me to come in, but not too far past the front door. She was very hesitant, and her voice sounded troubled as she told me there wouldn't be any more messages and therefore, no need for me to come back. I don't know what came over me just then, but I felt stunned, and I'm sure that's just how I looked. It was an emotional moment for The Lady, too, as she told me one more time, "Please do not come back, and if you ever see me again, please do not recognize me. This is very important!"

I was standing there staring at her. I did everything I could to keep from giving her an affectionate hug and kiss-something I really felt like doing, straight from the heart. I had a strong sense that she felt the same way. I told her I would abide by her wishes, and that I thought she was a very brave woman. As she closed the door, she had a tear in her eye and she told me I was also very brave. "Good luck to you, soldier," were her last words to me. I think I was as sad then as I had ever been in my life, and it was only then that I realized how sentimental a person I really was. I was concerned as to what would become of her, and still am. My time with her constituted a real and great adventure worthy of an epic movie, even if I didn't get to take the heroine in my arms and kiss her goodbye.

Johnny disappeared on the way back, but I made my way into the camp without any problems at the gate. I just stumbled along daydreaming about the Army, the war, the prison hospital, and of the poor wounded guys who were in my care (I mean, in the care of all the medics). It was hell, but I wouldn't take anything in the world for the experience. But, I sure as hell wouldn't want to do it again. I was fully conscious of the fact that it wasn't over yet.

Soon, some drastic changes befell us quite suddenly. No more wounded or soldiers or prisoners were coming into the camp, and once we had attended to the wounded already on hand, we started going out-right out of the camp. The guards had all taken off; not one was left, even Johnny whom we would have protected. This also meant no rations, which meant in turn that we had to go out scrounging on our own if we wanted to eat.

A couple of months earlier, on the way back to camp from a visit to The Lady, I had met a French couple from Brittany, Zaig and Pol Monjarret. Along with thousands of their countrymen, these two had been forced to witness the torching of their farm by German soldiers. Then, the Germans shipped them and all their possessions to Germany.

Now, Zaig and Pol were slave laborers in Ludwigsburg, working in the fields in the dead of winter with no protection whatsoever from the elements. It was a freezing cold night when I first ran into them. A moment before, I had been all alone; I remember walking over fields dotted with snow-covered haystacks. It must have been about five in the morning.

I froze in my tracks nearly paralyzed with fear when I spotted the two strangers. I gripped my pistol and for the first and only time released the safety. I realized when I got close enough to see them clearly that they weren't aggressors, although for a moment I had been sure that I'd run right into the Gestapo. The three of us sized each other up for a minute or so. They stared at me, trying to figure out my odd uniform. We were all shivering and sweating at the same time.

Zaig was clothed in a plain dress with a little floral print and only a navy cardigan sweater over that. She looked like a little girl with her hands shoved in her sweater pockets. She was pretty, but under the circumstances, she appeared quite plain. She wore no makeup and her hair was frazzled under her babushka. She spoke English very hesitantly, but she was better at it than she realized; even so, she kept excusing herself for her poor use of the language. Pol appeared taller than he really was. He must have been about five feet nine. He was a good looking man and was wearing an old suit jacket with mismatched pants that looked like hand-me-downs. His brown hair was combed straight back. As slave laborers, they had nothing, and were forced to live off the land.

On my next visit to The Lady, I asked her for some help for my new friends, and she gave me a few blankets, to which I added leftovers from my Christmas Red Cross parcel, including a little chewing gum which Zaig loved. Other than that, The Lady wanted nothing to do with them-she said she couldn't afford to get involved.

I met Pol and Zaig several more times after that when my guards didn't accompany me to or from The Lady's. I gave them no reason for my comings or goings and they didn't ask. They had dinners with some of the other slave laborers, and it turned out that some of them were members of the French Underground. When I learned of this, they signaled me with fingers to their lips that I needed to keep my mouth shut, and I did.

On the night of my final encounter with The Lady I ran into Pol and Zaig again. They now invited me to join them and some of their friends in the Underground who were holding what they called a feast. They took me to a house where there was a table laden with all kinds of food, and standing around the table were German women of all ages. It was quite a party-all the Frenchmen had women by their side, and one of them said to me that I could come back every night if I wanted, and they would find a girl for me, too if I'd like. A bit sheepishly, I answered that I had patients waiting for me in the Lazarett, and I'd better get back there in case I was needed.

Zaig and Polig Monjarret

Now, however, that the normal order of things had broken down, it occurred to me to seek out my French friends once again, who not only were chasing after every woman in the town, but were taking everything they could grab. While O-guns, cameras and field glasses seemed to be their favorites, they appeared to have a line on all the edibles in the area.

The next afternoon, I was standing the road with a few Frenchmen, watching unarmed German soldiers drifting by. It looked as if they had simply quit the war and just wanted to get home. I would swear that every one of them was over forty-five or fifty. Off in the distance, we saw a motorcycle with a sidecar coming toward us. One of my companions started taking pictures. It turned out that the driver of the motorcycle was the point man for the advancing French Battalion. He was just a little guy with a very happy face. He looked like he had just discovered the world. He and all the troops behind him were wearing American uniforms and helmets, but they turned out to be French.

They greeted us and were all gabbing away in French. I had a hard time getting their captain-a tall, handsome man-to listen to me. When he did turn to me, he spoke good English with only a slight accent. I told him of the Stalag and the hospital nearby, and that we needed help. He and a couple of his men came with me to look things over, but he proved unable to provide us with any medical supplies. He did say, though, that the Americans would be here in a day or so, and they were in charge.

In this picture: Sy (on the left), Zaig, and Pol (behind motorcycle man).

What the captain did next astonished me. He took me and an extremely skinny French kid (who looked as if a slight breeze might blow him over) to the first house down the road and knocked hard on the door. He told the poor women who answered, that she had to prepare a chicken dinner with a lot of potatoes and a salad, and have it ready by five o'clock. I was mightily struck by the tormented fright on the face of the woman and her teenage daughter. The captain was very stern and told them pointedly that he would have them shot if they didn't comply; just the way the Germans handled such matters with his people. I couldn't blame the captain, but I didn't want to face these two women again, so I told the French kid to find a friend and have the dinner themselves. I had seen too much German cruelty to want to benefit from French cruelty, I guess. All the while, I thought of Pol and Zaig and what had happened to them when the Germans had burnt down their farm and enslaved them. In spite of all the horrors we Americans had seen, were still pretty soft at the core.

I know this would not have been the case if the Germans had invaded and conquered our homeland. At that moment, I thought to myself that we Americans do not appreciate what or how much we have. I was suddenly in a rush to get back to the Lazarett for a very special dinner being prepared by an Indian prisoner who claimed to head chef of a famous Indian restaurant in London. He'd said that he'd been able to scrounge up all the ingredients he needed, including curry. Curry! That was the key word. I don't exactly know what came over me, but in light of all the starvation and near-starvation I'd witnessed, where so many of the sick men in my care had lost fifty pounds or so (and some a lot more), the thought of curry just overwhelmed me. The would-be chef was a large man with a mouth to match. Although he and the rest of the Indians had kept mainly to themselves in the camp, at this moment they were the only ones I could see in my mind's eye. I certainly hoped he wouldn't let me down now!

I was thinking of my Mom and Dad. Did they even know I was alive?

I was so proud to be an American; my feelings just welled up within me. Odd as it may seem, I felt sad knowing that not all Americans shared that feeling of what it meant to be free.

I experienced that sensation only two other times in my life: When I learned that Pearl Harbor had been bombed, and later, at the Wall in Jerusalem.

CHAPTER 26

Liberation Takes Shape: The French Depart

The French were leaving the camp in droves, and Alphonse de la Haye, the little Frenchman who had approached me in the bandage room long ago, found me to say a last goodbye, promising I would have pictures of all the events that had transpired. He told me that he appreciated my help and that I was a true comrade. He thanked me for being in the honor guard at all the French funerals. I asked him if he was the one who left the pistol on my table and he answered, "You must have more friends than you think." He presented me with a fine pair of military binoculars, a camera (for which I was unable to obtain any film), and some other sundry items, including a German bayonet. He stood at attention and once again said, "Goodbye, comrade," and kissed me on both cheeks. Then he saluted, did an about-face, and walked away. This short, small, meek-looking man looked as if he wouldn't step on an ant. Throughout his stay in the camp, he'd been wanted by the Germans, and they'd had him in their clutches without even knowing it. He was as good as his word. I have all the pictures that could have been taken, and they have afforded me many poignant memories of my past.

The Russian Problem

When I returned to the Lazarett, I found a few Russian soldiers waiting for me. They had come over from their section of the camp. We didn't think there were too many Russians in Stalag V-A since they were so well separated from the rest of us, and we'd never received any of their wounded. Still, we'd heard rumors of them, and we knew that there were at least a few Russians in the vicinity, but this was the first time I'd ever seen any of them. It was then and there, however, that we knew we'd soon have trouble with Russia. We told the leader of the Russian gang that the Amerikanskis were coming and to bug off, an expression we'd learned from the Brits and the Aussies, who were shoulder-to-shoulder with us on this issue.

One of them, whom I assumed to be an officer, started ordering us around, claiming they were going to take us back to Russia, and that we'd be OK. Another Russian prisoner had the nerve (we thought) to say how lucky we were now that the Germans had taken off, since Hitler had given an order to execute all P.O.W.'s before they could be liberated by Allied forces. We scoffed then, but we later learned that it was true; fortunately, the Kraut generals had ignored the order!

To get away from the Russkies, I quickly headed back to the French area, hoping to catch Pol and Zaig before they took off. Happily, I found them, just as they were getting ready to drive away in one of the cars their compatriots had confiscated. They appeared overjoyed at the prospect of heading back to France. The good-byes were very hard; most of us knew that we'd never see each other again.

Although I'd known Pol and Zaig for only a short while, we had gone through a lot together, and had grown quite close. They had greeted me almost every night when I was coming back to camp from The Lady's, and I felt as if we had a special bond between us that surpassed the usual bounds of friendship.

In our many conversations, I'd spoken mostly with Zaig, whose English was much more extensive than the tall, handsome Pol's. When Zaig and I spoke with one another, Pol usually looked down at the ground and drew shapes in the dirt with his toe. I often wondered if Pol might be jealous that I talked so much with his wife.

As we were about to part, Zaig thanked me for our friendship and kissed me warmly on both cheeks. Pol took my hand and shook it firmly between both of his. I couldn't believe this was happening, and happening so fast. An instant later-it seemed much longer than that at the time-I watched them get into the car they had commandeered and drive off. Zaig stuck her head out the window and waved as the car sputtered away with a great billow of dust rising up behind it.

Zaig Monjarret

The Americans Arrive

American forces hadn't yet made it to Stalag 5-A, but I'd heard from one of my French friends that if I rushed over to the center of Ludwigsberg, I'd see some GIs there. When I got to the main square, I encountered a large crowd of Germans who had surrounded a small group of American soldiers. The Germans were utterly jubilant, cheering the Yanks, jostling one another to get in close enough to pump their hands and slap them on the back. They certainly looked happy to see the Americans. I had arrived just in time to witness the lowering of the Nazi flag; within seconds, Old Glory was hoisted up the flagpole. With this beautiful sight before my eyes, I broke down completely and cried like a baby.

Only the thought of my mother and father helped me regain my composure. Did they even know I was alive? Never had I felt so proud to be an American, and yet I was sad at the same time, wishing that every American could share that feeling of what it meant to be free. How many of my countrymen actually appreciated their freedom? Did most Americans even know how lucky they were never to have faced an aggressive enemy on their home turf?

Above: Liberation picture. Sy proudly says "I'm an American."

Through the dense crowd I, caught sight of an American officer standing among his men. I tried to get his attention, but the enlisted soldiers around him wouldn't let me pass. Given how I was dressed, with an odd mix of American, French and Polish uniform parts, they refused at first to believe I was American; I guess this shouldn't have surprised me. I shouted at the top of my lungs, "Major, Major! I'm an American!" I held out my broken dog tags and my kriegie ID, and finally the GIs let me through. They looked so strong and powerful in their clean Army uniforms. It didn't even occur to me how gaunt and strange I must have looked to them.

The major looked tough, lean and fit, and said he knew about Stalag V-A. He told me his job was to get enough ambulances into the camp to evacuate the wounded and the sick, and to bring the medics out with them too. He climbed into a jeep and pulled me in after him, and we drove toward the camp. All this felt pretty damn good to me! On the road all the way back to the camp I saw GIs walking on both sides of the pavement, handing out cigarettes and other goodies to the throngs of Germans who had come out to greet them.

When we arrived at the Lazarett, I showed my major around. As we went through the bandage room, I pointed out the meager supplies with which I had to work over the past six months. He was amazed that I'd been able to provide any treatment at all for my patients. I introduced him to the other medics who were there, including Bruno and Alberti, who were trying to ready some of the patients for evacuation.

I told the major about Masa and his, "unwanteds," and how Masa had prevented the Germans from exterminating his pneumonia and TB patients. All the while, ambulances and trucks were streaming into the camp one after another. The prisoners who could, climbed onto the trucks; those who were too injured or ill to move out on their own were carried on stretchers to the waiting ambulances. One of the GIs gave me a duffle bag into which I packed all my things, including my surgical instruments. I wasn't about to leave those behind!

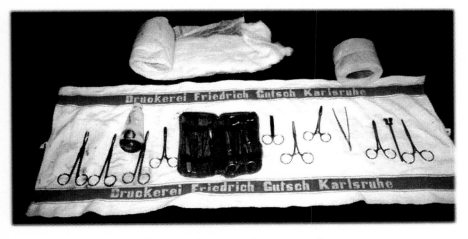

Above: Sy Brenner's surgery kit

The major and a captain and I were standing outside in front of the Lazarett when a British Chaplain from the main camp approached us. Despite the clear signs that he'd been living in lice-land since early in the war, the Chaplain was proud of his bearing and of his Brit uniform, and very proud to offer the newcomers a Raleigh cigarette, only to receive a rude wave-off from the American captain. "We don't smoke shit," bragged the captain with a smile. He took out a pack of Lucky Strikes and held them out for the Chaplain, whose face by this time had sunk to the ground. I felt like strangling him. The Chaplain had wanted to offer his liberators the highest compliment he could, a gift of the greatest, rarest wealth one could possess in a P.O.W. camp. "Here, smoke a Lucky, a real cigarette," said the captain. Fortunately, the major had the tact and good sense to try and save the moment. He threw the captain a disapproving look and presented the poor Chaplain with a chocolate bar, which he appeared pleased to accept.

Before he climbed into one of the ambulances, the major shook my hand warmly, and said, "I am very proud to have known you. I know you paid a hell of a price in this war. You did a hell of a job in a hell of a place for God and country. I'm putting you and that Japanese fella in for a Silver Star, or better." I was beaming from head to toe; I had never received such a compliment.

Being last one into the ambulance gave me the chance to look out the rear window as we drove off into a countryside laced with farms and valleys. We'd been on the road for what seemed a long time when bombed out buildings came into sight. Perhaps these were the suburbs of Stuttgart; wherever we were, all I could see was destruction all about. It reminded me of the railroad station at Freiberg, with shells of buildings and twisted steel standing straight up. I remembered the time the bombing had gone on for seventy-two hours straight: the earth had shaken so terribly I thought it would just open up around us.

We drove through Stuttgart, arriving a little later at an airfield where several C-47s had lined up, waiting to evacuate the P.O.W.'s. I helped some other medics get the wounded men onto the planes; after that, standing on the tarmac looking out over this corner of Germany, I was suddenly overcome by the most immense sense of relief, unlike anything I'd ever experienced before. Once again, I burst out in tears, this time when the wheels of the plane left the ground. I could hardly believe I was on my way to Rheims, France; my time in hell was falling away behind me.

My first days at home were very frustrating. I felt like a rookie at being a civilian. I felt lost and I couldn't get this or that, especially clothing. For three weeks I went searching for clothes. I had a very difficult time because of the shortage and because of my size.

CHAPTER 27

Almost Home

Arriving at Rheims, our group ended up at the 251st General Hospital, where medical personnel evaluated the state of our health. I was placed in a ward with my fellow medics from the Lazarett at Stalag V-A, including Bruno and Alberti. They, like me, could hardly believe we were finally out of the camp.

The staff took away our duffle bags with all of our gear and souvenirs. We were told we'd get them back before we left the hospital, but that we couldn't keep them with us on the ward. Then, the nurses deloused us-what a glorious feeling! Not until then did I notice I had shrunk to a mere ninety-seven pounds, and that I'd lost all my hair. The doctors diagnosed me as a malnutrition case, complicated by chronic diarrhea and stomach cramps. These symptoms persisted even when stuck to mild foods. I couldn't stop thinking about how much I wanted to tear into a big steak, but I'd have to put that off as long as the simple, nutritious hospital food continued to turn my poor guts inside out. It was also a great relief to get treatment for the wounds on my hands and face.

All in all, the hospital proved to be a fair place for our reintroduction to civilization. We were provided with lovely new toilet articles on a washcloth at our bedside, clean fresh pajamas, all the basic necessities. What we craved most, however, was paper and pencil with which to write to our loved ones. We were told that the Red Cross girls would get us what we wanted. The one who visited with me promised to bring me immediately stationery and a sharp pencil-my only desire. I never saw or heard from her again. One of the nurses ended up taking care of this for me, even offering to write my letters. Now, as had been the case in the camp, I felt sorriest for the married guys. While in the prison camp, they cried at times, wondering what was going on with their wives and families.

Some time later, hospital staffers ushered us into what looked like a small briefing room, complete with bulletin board and map. A skinny second lieutenant, probably fresh out of officer's school, strode in and called us to attention. We just stood there watching him as he watched us. Who among us was the most perplexed? We couldn't tell. One thing seemed sure-he did not know what to make of the gnarled less-than-100-pound wraiths who stood before him. After an uncomfortable period of silence, he said we didn't look to him like we could have been medics in the camp hospital. He then proceeded to read us the orders of the day, which included a list of the places in battle where each of us had been wounded. Next, with a highly gratifying tremble in his voice, the young officer awarded us all with Purple Heart medals. Did I see tears in his eyes as he pinned them to our chests? Finally, I was presented with a Bronze Star and a Combat Medic Badge, which meant more to me than any other medal I would receive.

While still in the hospital, a captain who said he was with S2 Army Intelligence interviewed all the medics from V-A. As I told him my story, he kept muttering, "Unbelievable. You guys are just unbelievable." I didn't know how much I should tell him about Alphonse and the resistance, or my meetings with The Lady, but I ended up relating pretty much my whole story. When I finally stopped talking, he whipped out an official-looking form and read me a direct order from it: "You are not to discuss what happened at Stalag V-A or what occurred in the Lazarett. You may not discuss it at any time, with any person. Is that understood?"

At this point, Bruno and I looked at each other, exchanging sarcastic glances. Bruno cleared his throat, as if about to say something, but the officer had already read his mind. "That information is classified," he said in response to the unasked question. That was it, all fixed and done. We couldn't believe it.

Before long, we began to act up. Life in the hospital proved pretty boring for men who were used to being so active, even as prisoners. Once, we started up a free-for-all pillow fight, but we quit that almost as soon as we had begun. Would you believe that we all had too much respect for pillows to throw them around? We weren't so shy about other foolishness, though, and liked to play it up in front of the nurses. I remember holding up my toothbrush when a nurse was looking me over, and shouting over to Bruno Galinski, "Hey, did you get one of these too? What do you think it's for?" To the next nurse on the scene one of the guys pointed to floor and told her not to slip on the ice. Bruno and I devised a charming act in which we would stand on our beds and snap our fingers at each other in various contorted positions. When the nurse asked us what we two clowns thought we were doing, we told her we were playing ping-pong.

May 8, V-E Day

May 8 was a big day for us-Victory in Europe! We were told that the war in Europe was officially over. All hell broke loose. Most of the men jumped out of the first-floor window of the hospital to run around the streets in their pajamas. I was most certainly among them. Some of the men got good and sick on the wine the French were distributing; I went that route, too.

Just a few blocks away from the hospital stood a schoolhouse, inside of which representatives of the German government signed the their declaration of surrender to the Allied forces. Little did I realize that at that very same moment, my parents received the telegram informing them that I was back under U.S. military control. That message turned out to be the first news they had of me since they had learned I was missing in action back in November.

They were happy beyond words, as was I-happy in the knowledge I'd be going home soon. My comrades and I had all been through so much; I couldn't help but think over and over again about our ordeals in the camp; my time in the Verbandzimmer, and the operations I had performed on so many men, all without having had any medical training at all! Whitey was never far from my mind, but so were the others; how frightened I was that what I had done for them (or to them) would affect them for the rest of their lives. I remembered my experience as Man of Confidence, how I'd helped that lieutenant get back his bars. I remembered with some fondness planning the Christmas party for the men. I thought about dear Pol and Zaig returning home to their destroyed house and farm. How would they manage to pick up the pieces from here, of course, I thought a lot about The Lady. Although we had said so little to one another during my visits to her house, she had touched me in a way that even now I could hardly imagine, especially considering the harsh treatment that was the way of life in the prison camp.

Finally, I couldn't help but think a lot about home. My buddies and I smoked a lot of cigarettes in the hospital, and this served as a constant reminder to me of my father, who was a pretty heavy smoker himself. I remembered how cold it was during wintertime at home and how my father's cigarettes sometimes froze to his lips. God, how homesick I was!

On this day of days, V-E Day, back in the hospital, a group of us were standing around Bruno's bed joking around when I noticed John Alberti with a most odd expression on his face. He was staring at the medical chart hanging on the end of my bed. The information there really wasn't any of his business, but that didn't bother me much at the moment. Out of the blue, he shouted, "Hey Bruno! What's this 'H' mean on Brenner's chart?" No matter that I was standing right there, Bruno called back, "'H' is for Hebrew. Brenner's Jewish."

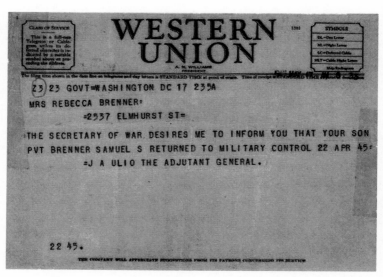

Above: Telegram sent to Sy Brenner's family informing he was back under U.S. military control.

I'll never forget what happened next. Alberti's skin positively blanched as he turned to me; he had a grotesque scowl on his face. Then he simply walked away without saying another word. I remembered standing next to him at the Easter service, only a few short weeks before. Back then we'd recited the 23rd Psalm together and he'd said, "Isn't it wonderful they let us do this?" I had replied, "Yes, it certainly is." With that we'd become friends. Ever since then, Alberti had followed me around just about all day long, talking with me about any and every subject that came into his mind. He was a short guy with a pencil-thin mustache and a sallow complexion who didn't mix well with the other men. On an earlier occasion one of the guys had said to me that Alberti was kind of creepy looking, but it wasn't until this day in the hospital that I realized how creepy he really was, and how ugly was his anti-Semitism. Because I was Jewish, Alberti would never speak to me again, now that he knew the terrible truth about me. Here was just one more wrenching feeling that stuck with me for the rest of my life.

Not quite four weeks later, June 2nd to be precise, I transferred to Camp Lucky Strike, where thousands of other P.O.W.'s received preparation for the journey home. So excited was I, that I didn't even realize it was my birthday. At Lucky Strike we received new uniforms and supplies. While we were here, the camp administrators tried to fatten us up a bit for the trip home; I guess they didn't want the folks back home to see us as the scarecrows we'd become. One thing was for sure-the food was a lot better at this place. Imagine how beautiful a slice of white bread with butter looked to me now! Our greatest disappointment at Lucky Strike occurred when we got our duffle bags back. My buddies and I were distraught to learn they had been looted-almost all of the things we had taken out of Germany were missing.

Then, one day, we were loaded aboard a hospital ship for the trip back to the States. This crossing proved to be much better than the one coming over. We didn't experience any storms and we didn't have to witness any tankers getting blown up. It was much more comfortable, all in all. Now, they really tried to fatten us up. The crew kept serving us malted milk over and over throughout the day along with all kinds of other rich foods. It got to be sickening, to the point I felt like throwing up if I even smelled malted milk. But all this had its intended effect; I gained thirteen pounds on that luxury cruise. Finally, we arrived at Fort Miles Standish near Boston, just in time for lunch.

Once on shore, we filed into a big building that was mess hall, where stood in line for what seemed an eternity, waiting to be fed once again. Then a near-riot broke out when one of the ex-P.O.W.'s asked a passing kitchen helper what was causing the delay. We learned that we were waiting for German P.O.W.'s to finish their ice cream!

My dysentery problem was worse, not better, so the authorities put me in the base hospital, in a four-bed ward. There were two other men in the room, both from the South. Now I experienced again at first-hand something I had seen back when I was in training in Louisiana: one of the men was white and the other black. The white fellow was the younger, even younger than I. He sheepishly asked me if I would read his letter to him and sit on his bed while doing so, because he didn't want , "the nigger boy to hear."

The black kid's bed was across the aisle from mine. When I finished reading the letter I remembered all the Southern boys I had know back in basic training who couldn't read or write. The white soldier didn't even thank me for my trouble; he just said he wished to hell they'd get that, "nigger boy out of there." He had no right to be there. He then started calling the poor guy all kinds of names.

For my part, I was happy to share my room, time and friendship with any honest soul, and was just as happy to converse with my roommates, black and white. I asked the black kid how long he'd been in the hospital, only to be interrupted by the other guy, who blurted out, "Why do you want to talk to that black son of a bitch?" I answered, "He served his country and deserves the same respect as anyone else!" I couldn't believe my ears when he came right back at me said, I sounded just like, "one of those damned Jews." So, I asked him if he knew any Jews. Did he know what they looked like? Did they have horns?

The white boy looked at me quizzically and said, "Yeah. I never met a Jew, but I heard they did have horns, come to think of it." I told him curtly that he was meeting one now, and if he didn't shut up I'd kick the shit out of him. I never said another word to him for the next two days that I was there, and he didn't say anything more to the black kid. It seems I had become very sensitive to racism.

While I was in the hospital at Fort Miles Standish (and for that matter, for the past eight months), I had worried that my parents never received the letter that had been in my greatcoat pocket. I still didn't know my mother had suffered a heart attack-something I only learned when I was allowed to call home from the hospital.

Believe it or not, all the time I was there, my favorite activity was to stand on a street corner and watch the trolley cars go by and listen to their bells clanging. Strange as it may seem, that was the most beautiful sound in the world to me just then.

CHAPTER 28

Homeward Bound

I had requested a furlough, but the doctors refused because the diarrhea was still pretty bad. So, instead of sending me home, they shipped me to Fort Sheridan, Illinois on the ninth of June. This at least brought me a little closer to home. My other physical problems, including the stomach pains, continued to plague me. At Sheridan, they placed me in a dispensary which had a small ward, where a nurse administered a regimen of medications. I only saw a doctor once-right after I had arrived there. I finally convinced the nurse to talk to someone in authority about obtaining a furlough so I could go home for a while.

One day, I was digging through my poor belongings and came across the dog tags that I had taken off the dead man with whom I'd been locked in the closet for three days. Foolishly, I asked one of the nurses if I might dictate a letter to the dead man's wife, and she agreed. In the letter, I told her of her husband's death and where he had been buried. Not until after I mailed it did it occur to me that the man might not have been married, but I found comfort in the thought that his parents might have received the letter, and in that, would perhaps have found some solace. I put my home address on the envelope, but no one ever wrote me back. Even now, I wonder how his family must have felt, or how they took my letter, assuming anyone who knew him ever read it. Before I left Fort Sheridan, I gave the dog tags to a major who appeared to be in charge of such things, and he said he'd take care of it, whatever that meant.

I was getting increasingly nervous by the day. I wanted so badly to see my family and to feel something again of my old self. I know that I was making it miserable for the doctor and nurses at Fort Sheridan. Finally, after making me promise to take the medication faithfully he had prescribed for me on the exacting schedule specified, the doctor relented. He made arrangements for me to obtain all the medicines I needed, and told me that if I failed to follow his instructions, I'd end up in the hospital or worse.

As soon as I could get to a pay phone, I called my parents. My mother answered and began to cry hysterically as soon as she recognized my voice; luckily, my sister Rae was there, and she took the receiver from my mom. Rae started crying, too when I told her I'd be home early the next day. By now, I couldn't wait to leave. I took a bus from Fort Sheridan to the railroad station and got a ticket on an overnight train to Chicago. Having gotten to the station several hours early, I thought I'd be ready for sleep on the long train ride, but in fact, I didn't sleep a wink.

A whole lifetime before, or so it seemed, my brother, Saul had driven me to the station when I departed for my Army training. Now, Saul was there waiting to pick me up. All the same folks who had seen me off were there with him-my mom, dad and sister Rae, who couldn't wait another minute to see me. Within seconds of catching sight of each other, we were all crying.

My mother looked very frail. The years had taken their toll on her, and all her worry over me and my brother, Myer had only compounded the effect of the heart attack she had suffered simultaneous with my capture. I had never seen my father in tears before; he rarely showed any emotion unless he was smiling. I gave him a great big hug-the first of many to come in the future. Then, with a smile I showed him my little knife. I said, "You were right. Sometimes a little knife is better than a big one." My sister Rae, despite a lot of tragedy that had occurred in her life, was all smiles. My brother Saul, who had brought me toys now and then when I was a young kid, was there for me now too.

My folks had put on their best clothes in honor of my return. My mother was wearing a little black straw hat and a dark print dress with a white Peter Pan collar. I said, "Ma, you didn't have to get all dressed up for me." She laughed and said, "I knew you would come back," and then we were all crying again, including my father. He too was all dressed up in what was probably the only suit he owned, topped off in a dark gray felt hat.

My sister, Rae wore a light summer dress. I was more than a little alarmed, though, by the sight of a large gauze bandage wrapped all around her right arm, from wrist to elbow. She had been accidentally scalded by a kettle of boiling water. She was to have gone to the doctor that morning to have the bandage changed, but she'd told him that her brother, the Army medic was coming home that day, and he could change it. And I did. I boiled my Verbandzimmer instruments, removed the dead skin, applied some ointment, and re-bandaged the arm. That marked the last time in fifty years I ever cleaned or used those instruments.

Saul was dressed in slacks and an open-necked shirt, and he looked very tired. He said, "The rest of the family is out at the lake. Would you like to go out there too? It's so hot and humid in the city, and it's only for the weekend." I replied, "Seeing that it's only Friday, why not? But, do they have any streetcars out there?" Saul thought that was a pretty peculiar question, so I explained about my desire to hear the clanging of streetcar bells.

My parents had moved while I'd been away, and now the two of them lived in a small flat on the second floor of a four-family complex. As we were driving home, I enjoyed the sights of old familiar places, and I couldn't help but notice that everyone restrained themselves from asking questions or talking, although I felt that all eyes were on me. Saul drove past my old alma mater, Northern High School, of which I had many fond memories. I'd been a member of the Radio Club, had the lead in the senior play, as well as being on the baseball team.

I'd met my first real girlfriend at Northern, Celia Weiner, who had the lead opposite me in the senior play. She was a very sweet girl, and had been my prom date. My brother Myer had loaned me his brand new, fire-engine red Dodge, and we had a great time. After the prom we'd gone to a popular place called Bill's Hideout that had food and dancing. Our crowd sat at a table that had a wall telephone. It kept ringing and no one from Bill's answered it, so my friend Bob Ellis picked it up and said, "Jerkowitz Funeral Home." Bob always got away with pranks like that.

Right then, in the midst of what was surely the most poignant moment of my entire life before and since, I remembered one of the sillier events of my high school career-a stunt I pulled on my favorite teacher: Mr. S.M. Horton, who taught sociology, would never tell us his first name, referring to himself only by his initials. On a Friday night, the brilliant idea occurred to me to look him up in the telephone book, where I discovered his first name was Sumner. Now, of course, I had his phone number as well, and I couldn't resist the urge to give him a call. I was very good at speaking in various dialects (in fact I still am today), so I put on my best rural-hick voice and told him when he answered that I was Mr. Jones from Railway Express, and that we had a crate of eggs for him in our office. "And since we don't deliver on weekends and we ain't got refrigeration," I said, "You'd better come down right away and pick 'em up."

"Who'd be sending me eggs?" Mr. Horton inquired in a surprised voice. "I don't know, sir, but they'll spoil by Monday," I replied. The perfect straight man, Mr. Horton then asked, "Where did they come from?" And I answered, "From a chicken's ass, you damn fool!" Monday, when we went back to school no one said a thing until I was leaving his classroom, when Mr. Horton walked up to me, gave me a penetrating gaze from over the top of his glasses, and said, "Brenner, how long have you worked for Railway Express?"

My next random reminiscence took me back to the senior play, which suddenly seemed to me as if it might have been an omen of my future. Its title was, "Three Live Ghosts," which had been released in movie form a few years before. It was about three prisoners of war in World War I who had escaped and wound up in the home of the character I played-a soldier believed by his family and sweetheart to have been killed in combat. My sister, Rae broke the silence that engulfed us in the car after we had passed the school, and said, "I guess seeing your old high school brought back some memories. I guess you had it pretty bad. How did they treat you?" With a quizzical look on her face she asked, "Did they know you were Jewish?"

I had anticipated questions about my P.O.W. experience and was hoping to avoid them, but here it was, right at the start of my new life. I didn't feel much like talking about it yet, and I truly believed that even my own family and friends weren't ready to hear about it, especially my mother. So I told Rae she was correct seeing the school brought back happy memories. And for the next forty-five years I never spoke about my time as a P.O.W.. To those who knew I'd been in a prison camp and asked about it, I said they'd never believe me anyway. My family-my parents and siblings, and later my wife and children-never knew of my wartime travails. Not until 1988, when I received a special Prisoner of War Medal at the Marine Corps Recruit Depot in San Diego, did they ever learn about what I'd done during the war.

So, I never did answer Rae's question; I just told her how much I had enjoyed the tobacco she'd sent me, and how I'd smoked the pipe upside down, because the enemy could see a lighted cigarette a mile away and then shell our position. With a huge smile on his face, my father said, "See, even if it was only smoking a pipe, taught you something useful after all." My mother said something that she'd always said when I was a boy: "You learn something every day."

When we got to the house, my mother had a nice lunch waiting. But, I felt very badly when I had to tell her that I couldn't eat any vegetables at all, whether raw or cooked or fruit or roughage of any kind. After lunch, we took off for Cass Lake, where my sister Clara, and her husband, Lou Newman, had a very large and comfortable cottage right on the shore.

"In war the result is never final."
(Carl von Clausewitz)

CHAPTER 29

A Serviceman's Readjustment Acts

Cass Lake was about forty-five miles from Detroit, and it took us what seemed like an eternity to get there. On the way, Saul and Rae caught me up on the news of the family. My mother-the proudest grandmother that ever lived-took over the conversation when it turned to my nieces and nephews, some of whom were born while I was away. I learned from my brother that he had notified the Red Cross when word arrived that I was missing in action, and that the Red Cross, in turn, helped to arrange an emergency leave for Myer so he could come home from the Pacific and take care of my mother after she'd suffered her heart attack on the night I'd been wounded. Myer had never had a furlough since the war began. When home, the Detroit papers ran some very nice stories about him and the Samura sword he'd brought with him, which he'd put on display in the window of Detroit's largest department store, J.L. Hudson Company.

Passing through Keego Harbor, the metropolis with exactly one stoplight to its name, I was filled to overflowing with nostalgia as we drove by the Keego Theatre, the old gas station, and Strong's Pavilion-a skating and dancing establishment where I'd passed many happy hours. When we arrived at the cottage, the rest of my family that could be there drew us into an exceptionally wonderful weekend of laughter and tears. People in the area must have thought we were crazy, although I suppose that uncounted thousands of families across the country must have experienced the same kind of reunions at just about the same time that we did. Some of Clara and Lou's neighbors came by to say hello, but it was much more fulfilling for me to meet up with my nieces and nephews, some of them for the very first time. Everyone kept asking me how it was, "over there," but they soon realized I didn't want to talk about it. The only part of my story I could easily articulate had to do with the Russians, with whom I believed we'd soon have real trouble. In quiet moments, I kept thinking about poor old Myer, still in the Pacific, and my nephew Alan somewhere in the wild blue yonder.

I truly enjoyed the feeling I got from seeing everyone dressed in bathing suits and play clothes, just like in the old days. The cottage was full of people, and Clara and Lou were perfect hosts, to a fault, especially when their friends brought friends with them. The cottage was large and airy, and quite conducive to the social events of the day. It had four large bedrooms upstairs, a large kitchen, a huge dining room and living room, and gracious verandah that circled the house, all furnished appropriately for the place and season. Outside, was a large and well-manicured lawn that extended about fifty feet to the water, ending with a foot and a half drop to a stony beach. There were a couple of small boats tied up just offshore.

I can hardly describe the terrific time I had that weekend, swimming, boating, playing catch with some of the nephews who were growing up on me. What a sensation it was to perform these simple acts with the gear that so many American young people took for granted, by which I mean a baseball, a bat, a mitt-things that been out of my reach for what seemed now like years.

My parents sat on wicker chairs watching us; I can still see the little smiles on their faces. As we would have said in Yiddish, they, "kvelled." They were so proudly gleaming at the sight of their youngest son playing with their grandchildren. What a weekend! Full of affection, happiness, kissing, hugging and laughter, all in very stark contrast to the gross inhumanity and loss of dignity that I had experienced a couple of months before.

All the way home, late on Sunday, my mother held on to my arm very tightly, sobbing quietly from time to time and dabbing at her eyes with a hanky she took from her purse. When she'd opened her handbag to search for her hanky, I noticed some of my letters to her from the camp crumpled up at the bottom. When I asked her if she'd been carrying those around with her all the time, she said she had. Moreover, she told me of a vow she'd made to God if he would bring me home alive-to cook seven days a week for the boys at the Chachmy Lubin Yeshiva, an Orthodox Jewish seminary school near our home. I had never harbored any doubts about Ma's deep piety or commitment to her spiritual life, but this amazed me anyway, and I said so. With a casual hand gesture toward heaven, as if to say that this was really nothing, she brought the conversation right back down to earth and complained that I was too skinny and that my complexion was sallow. She told me I needed to get some sun and some exercise. Thank God she didn't see me when I was down to ninety-seven pounds! No one was ready to comment on the loss of my hair, and I was sure grateful for that.

Above: Mr. and Mrs. Brenner

When we got home, she wanted to give me a good, healthy meal, but I had to beg off. I had a hard time talking her out of it, telling her I was so tired and that I needed to go to bed. What a joy it was to enter my own bedroom and fall into a nice clean bed that smelled so fresh. There was my own pillow sitting on top of a real bed, and not that grimy dirty burlap sack filled with straw and crawling with lice. In the morning, after my father left for work, I spent two hours in the bathroom. I wasn't primping and preening, however, but suffering the ill effects of the good food I'd eaten over the past few days, which was running right through me. I was soon embarrassed for having to spend so much time in the bathroom.

While still in the bathroom that morning, I smelled the aroma of fresh brewed coffee-another experience that brought me right back to my childhood, when I used to go to the grocery store with my mother and stand next to the fresh coffee as it came out of the grinder. I walked into the kitchen and saw my mother with a very concerned look on her face. I knew she understood the situation and was trying to figure out what I could eat. We decided we would try a little tomato juice, a couple of soft-boiled eggs and some dry toast. That seemed to do the trick, for a little while anyway.

As I finished my breakfast, a telegram arrived from Fort Sheridan, advising me that I was to report to the Sands Hotel in Miami Beach by the following Monday. This message confirmed news we had received while still aboard the hospital ship: all prisoners of war would take R & R at resorts either in California or Florida; the choice was ours to make. Silly as this may sound, at that moment the movie, "Moon over Miami" had entered my thoughts, and it was because of that I chose Florida. Now I was quite surprised the orders had come through so fast.

Later that day, I was standing on the upstairs porch just staring at the surroundings and thinking to myself how lucky I was, but I still didn't hear the clanging of the streetcar bells, as I so dearly desired. While I'd been overseas, Detroit's streetcars had disappeared, only to be replaced by buses-a great disappointment to me, to be sure! In the midst of my reverie, a car drove up to the house, and I saw Big Bernie Trubowitz's mother and father climb out. I was so excited, I almost jumped off the second-floor porch, but I thought better of it and ran downstairs to greet them with tears in my eyes. I gave both of them big hugs and kisses. Even though Bernie and I were very close, I had never seen fit to show such affection to him or his family; for that matter, the same was true with most of my school chums-we knew each other's parents, but the parents weren't necessarily well acquainted with their sons' friends' parents. But when all the letters started coming back M.I.A. and K.I.A., my friends' parents rallied around my folks, creating in effect a support group that worked remarkably well and provided them with a lot of comfort. The afternoon with the Trubowitz's was great. We had coffee and cookies and a lot of conversation about all the guys and where they were.

After Mr. and Mrs. Trubowitz left, I decided to call all of my friends' parents and thank them for the warmth they'd shown my family. One by one, they all wanted me to come over to visit, but just then I didn't feel strong enough to go through all the emotional stress such occasions were sure to produce. I told them I would see them in a couple of weeks after my R & R in Miami, not knowing at that time that I wouldn't be back for several months.

At that moment, all I wanted was to be alone with my thoughts and not have to answer a lot of well meaning questions, such as, "How was it? You must have had a terrible time. What happened to your hair? You're so skinny; you should have another piece of cake." The fact of the matter was I didn't want to talk about it, and as I learned later, most all of the other ex-prisoners of war felt exactly the same way. We were all sure that no one would believe us in any event, even if we did talk.

Our phone rang early that evening, and it was my sister, Clara on the other end. She said the family was going to gather at her house a little later on and that we should come over, too. Although I thought it a little odd to have a family function on a Monday evening, I was glad when my brother-in-law, Max picked my father, mother, and me up. He and my sister Fanny had a shiny black Plymouth that appeared to be brand new; it even smelled new. Fanny told me I ought to feel honored to ride in such a fine equipage-one of the last cars Plymouth built before converting to war production. Fanny and Max had kept it in the garage throughout most of the war because Max needed to keep all his gas-ration coupons for his truck, which was necessary for his roofing and tinning business. On the way to Clara and Lou's, he told me the car was mine as long as I was home, and the gas tank was full.

Even now, Max liked to tease me as if I were a young kid. He would tell me something, and "I'd ask, why?" He would answer, "Just because." He still called me by my Jewish name Schmuel, which he always intoned as part of a joke he'd been telling for twenty years-that my mother had found me on a farm and therefore I was Schmuelikel (the Yiddish diminutive form of Schmuel) from the farm.

When we got to Clara and Lou's, the whole family was there, as well as two older couples and a young lady whom I immediately figured had been invited as a kind of blind date for me. No one said anything about my hair loss except for the mysterious young lady, who kept telling me that if I mixed kerosene with a little olive oil and rubbed in on my scalp three or four times a day, my hair would grow back! I tried to stay away from her for the rest of the evening, but every time she caught my eye she would repeat her story about restoring my hair. I did all I could to maintain my composure, but it wasn't easy.

The real surprise of the evening came when my family members pulled out all the letters and packages they had sent me while I'd been a P.O.W.. These items had been returned to sender, with all kinds of markings written or stamped on them in exactly the same order: "Searching," "missing," presumed K.I.A.." And they'd all been signed by Captain Jack Pearson, who was one of the first officers I could remember in the service company when I had joined the Army. He'd been a 2nd Lieutenant back then. I didn't have the chance to go through all the letters that evening, but I had a ball tearing into the packages. They were all full of crumbs from stale cookies and cakes and there were more than a few razors and blades. I found small salami in one box, and I thought how welcome that would have been in the camp. My sister, Rae had sent me package after package with a pound of my favorite pipe tobacco inside; how I wished I'd had my pipe while I was a prisoner. Throughout this most pleasant ritual, the strange girl kept insisting that I anoint my head with kerosene and olive oil. I promised myself I'd never see her again.

I thoroughly enjoyed the rest of the evening in the company of my family who seemed by now to realize that I didn't want to talk about the war. Once I felt tempted to say, "I heard you had a very tough time while was away," but thought the better of it. It made my heart glad to see my mother and father sitting at the dining room table, taking it all in, smiling and exchanging comments as they drank their tea in the old-country style in a glass, with a spoon in the glass and a cube of sugar between their teeth.

I had a guilty conscience using Max's car because gasoline was still so scarce, so I didn't take it out very much. I spent most of the next few days at Saul's tire shop, writing up his bank deposits and changing tires. When things got slow, I listened to the old-timer who re-grooved old tires so they could go a few more miles; new tires were not yet available on the market. This old fellow liked to spin yarns about the good old days in the tire business and this caused me to wonder if I would ever spin yarns about my good old days. Here I am doing it!

I was quite tempted to ask out the cute blonde girl who worked at the bank. I made it a point to go to her window every day. She was making eyes at me and I certainly felt attracted to her, but I just didn't feel confident about going out on a date. With very good reason, I was still afraid of getting cramps and diarrhea, and that just wouldn't have made for much of an evening on the town.

At the urging of my family, I did call up one of the girls I had dated before I'd gone into the Army, whose name was Betty. Her mother answered the phone and then screamed at me. "You have a lot of nerve asking a married woman out!" I was embarrassed, and I wondered how many others of the girls I used to date were married by now.

A soldier came into the tire store and told me about a great bar not far from there where one was sure to find a lot of girls, good music and dancing. Although bars were never my thing, and I'd have to limit my drinking to club soda, I thought I might give Connie's Bar a try. As I walked in, I noticed how well lighted it was, compared to the rest of the blacked out city. The soldier I'd met was right-the music was loud, the place was positively overflowing with pretty girls, and there were servicemen from every branch of the armed forces. Some were very drunk, and most were trying to have a good time. I noticed a civilian dressed in a tuxedo, wandering around with an air of authority. He looked about ten feet tall to me and had black hair graying at the temples-a regular tough mug who could have played a gangster in the movies. He milled around making his presence known and every so often checked with the bartender.

I finally got up enough courage to ask a good-looking blonde girl to dance. She was sitting at a table with two other young ladies. I was never much of a dancer, but we seemed to hit it off pretty well and spent the rest of the evening together. I asked her if I could take her home, but she hesitated because she'd come with her girlfriends. Since they all lived in the same area, I offered to take them home too-much better than taking the bus. Max's shiny black Plymouth looked like a limo to them. Of course, I took my new friend home after dropping off the others. We had a most enjoyable evening making love in the back seat of Max's car. This was the first time I ever gave a thought about being bald at the age of twenty-three. After that, it didn't bother me; I was sure it was better to have no hair at all and be alive than being dead with a full head of hair.

The next day, one of my old gang, Dave Eisman, came home on furlough. As I was soon to leave for Miami, Dave and I decided to find dates and go out that evening. We went to a club called Lee and Eddie's where they had name entertainment and dancing. The place was jammed with people, and we were lucky to get a table up front. The waitress seemed friendly, and seeing that we were servicemen, she suggested a ten-dollar bottle of champagne. We had a very nice time until we got the bill-forty bucks for the bottle! Dave, normally a quiet and reserved person, turned red as a beet and let out a loud "What?" I cried out even louder, "What is this place, a clip joint?" People could hear us all the way across the room.

The waitress explained that they were all out of the ten-dollar bottles, and I replied that we should have been informed. She asked us to wait a minute while she got the manager. Well, who should walk up, in a tux, but the guy from Connie's Bar? He didn't know me, but I recognized him right away. Seeing that I was the loudmouth, he leaned down close to my ear and said in an unmistakably threatening tone, "The bill is forty dollars and you will pay for it."

I got up from my chair very quickly, and on the way up, my head brushed his chin, pushing him back. I told him the story in a very loud voice and then asked him if he played bait-and-switch on all the servicemen. I had a ten-dollar bill in my hand and gave it to him. He grabbed it said, "I'm going to remember you." I said back to him in an even louder voice that I already remembered him from Connie's Bar. I never went back there, either. As we left, Dave said to me, "You got pretty tough since you were a kid." Little did he know that in the last couple of years, I'd dealt with far tougher men than that. I felt good telling that guy off.

My orders instructed me to rest and have a good time.

CHAPTER 30

Beautiful Miami

Monday morning, my brother, Saul drove me down to the railway station for my trip to glamorous Miami. I had neglected to make a reservation for a Pullman car, and because the train was so crowded I was, lucky to get a seat at all; believe it or not, a lot of people were left standing.

I felt excited to be going to such a posh place as the Sands Hotel at the Army's expense-hardly the usual Army experience. Myer had left me some money, and I made sure to bring that with me; I was determined to follow orders!

On board the train, I sat next to a young woman from Georgia who had the cutest southern drawl. I loved her accent and all the peculiar regional expressions she had for any subject. She was pretty with blue eyes, and she wrinkled her nose as she started every sentence with a, "y'all." There were a lot of servicemen on the train, and we had a very good time singing and joking around. Here again I was entranced as the train passed through cities I thought I'd never have the opportunity to see. The conductor announced that due to a problem on the track we'd have a three-hour layover when we pulled into Atlanta. He instructed us not to go too far from the train in case they repaired the problem more quickly than that, and once we were rolling again the engineer would try to make up for lost time. A little while later, we learned the nature of the, "problem: thousands of people in and around Atlanta were running around, celebrating wildly blocking roads, bridges and railroad tracks; the government of Japan had just declared its unconditional surrender to the Allied forces! Today, August 14, 1945, would be known forever after as V-J Day! Needless to say, we had a celebration of our own on the train.

The little Georgia Peach who was my seat-mate told me there was a very good restaurant right near the station where we could get the best chili in the whole world. Having never heard of chili before I was a bit embarrassed, but wishing to represent myself as a gentleman of the North, I gallantly said, "Great! Let's go." She sprang from her seat, grabbed my hand, and said, "Stick with me." She led me out of the station and down the block to the chili parlor, which bore a sign over the door that spelled out "Chili Pot." While we were waiting to be served, her stomach started gurgling, and without blinking an eye she said, "Hush now, your daddy's in the Navy."

Now much to my dismay, I found out what the best chili in the world tasted like and as soon as I started to eat it, I knew the best chili in the world was going to have a problem with my stomach; I also knew who the new father was. My companion tried to talk me into staying over in Atlanta, but my stomach and I were all fired up to get to Miami Beach as soon as we could. The rest of the trip, I spent in the men's room meditating on the high price I was paying for a taste of the world's best chili.

I shared a cab to the hotel with another GI when we arrived in Miami the next evening. The driver told us ours was the newest hotel on the beach, the last one to be completed before the war. Beautiful as it was, I found it hard to imagine it was now operated by Uncle Sam. We checked in, and I noticed immediately that the desk clerk bell man and all the other employees were wearing military uniforms. Nice duty if you could get it!

How surprised and pleased I was to learn that I didn't have to share a room with anyone; that was a very good thing, because a roommate would never have had the chance to get into the bathroom. The hotel had a fine dining room and a menu that seemed unimaginable for an Army installation. felt, for the moment at least, that I might settle in for a most enjoyable couple of weeks.

All the other, "guests" in the hotel were ex-P.O.W.'s. As we sat around the lounge in search of a little conversation, we found we could indeed talk to one another, understand each other and otherwise believe what each other had to say-a far cry from what we'd experienced at home just days earlier. We learned that we had all felt pretty much the same when we'd arrived home-we just didn't want to talk about it, and we didn't think people, even our family and close friends, would believe us. Here, however, we felt completely free to open up to each other; in fact, you might have called us a private club. It was a great relief to me to learn that I wasn't the only one who had to excuse himself suddenly and run to the toilet.

We felt very badly for one of the ex-P.O.W.'s who came home to find his wife living with another man. This guy needed a lot of help, but it wasn't the kind we could give him. His wife had claimed that she thought he was dead. We heard a lot of stories like that.

The next morning, I came face to face with the most sumptuous breakfast buffet I could imagine. Anything and everything I might have wanted to eat was laid out on great tables in the most tempting way possible. I adopted safety and sensibility, however, as the order of the day and settled for two soft-boiled eggs, toast and coffee. Just for today, I told myself. I feared even the fresh, lovely Florida orange juice, and I know that was smart thinking. I spent the morning on the beach and took a tour of the city in the afternoon, throughout which my guts stayed reassuringly quiet.

I enjoyed thoroughly the nice nap I took before dinner; then I went downstairs and tucked into a steak and lobster tail combo with French fries and a generous wedge of chocolate cake, followed by coffee. The salads looked good, but I knew well enough by now that fruits and vegetables ran right through me. I also stayed away from the soups, delicious though they looked. I have a feeling that most of the other ex-P.O.W.'s stayed away from the soups, too, because we weren't quite able yet to forget the ghastly concoctions served us by our last hosts, which contained such tasty nutriment as seaweed, grass, maggots, and if we were lucky, a few potato peels. This would surely be a heavenly two weeks, with, "no drunks or women allowed," according to the sign in the lobby.

I remembered my friend, Bob Feldman's parents used to come to Miami for part of each year, and wanting to say hello to them, I thought I could find the hotel where they usually stayed. It turned out to be a much longer walk than I'd anticipated, and the combination of heat and humidity just about wore me out. I finally arrived at the Hotel Edison only to learn that the Feldmans weren't in residence. I immediately lowered my profusely perspiring body into a lounge chair and drifted off into a lovely daydream involving my distant past-Montreal, my parents, my brother-in-law, Max-when I noticed a short but shapely woman with darkish blond hair staring at me. I suppose I must have looked somewhat out of place surrounded as I was by a throng of the hotel's usual patrons, most of whom looked to be sixty or older. The young woman addressed me by someone else's name, and I was sorry to tell her I wasn't who she thought I was. "I guess I was stood up," she replied. "I was supposed to meet a guy here."

I asked her if she'd like to take in a movie, but she said she was sorry, but had to be somewhere else at a certain time. She did give me her name and address, and we made a date for lunch the next day.

She greeted me at the door when I got to her apartment, and then surprised me by telling me to make myself comfortable while she went out on a short errand. This didn't feel quite right to me, as if she were setting me up for something. I sat down for a few minutes but then got antsy. I started to wander around the apartment, looking out the window, and then past the open door to her bedroom. Her open closet door caught my attention right away; hanging on the rack was a whole row of little girl's dresses. I may have been mistaken, but I couldn't help but think of the guy back at my hotel who had just received a Dear John letter. That had affected him so deeply. At the same time, I remembered all the guys in my unit and in the camp who had to endure that kind of treatment from their loved ones. I felt for every one of them. Some of the married men who had been jilted became reckless in battle and acted as if they wanted to die. I decided to get the hell out of there and went back to the Sands Hotel, where I had lunch alone and felt much the better for it.

Bailing out of my date turned out to be a good idea, because I became nauseated that afternoon and suffered a dreadful, seemingly endless attack of diarrhea. I went on sick call, and that was the end of my not-quite-three-days stay at the glamorous Sands Hotel.

An olive-drab command car picked me up (ironically, a similar model to my brother-in-law, Max's Plymouth) and took me on a long ride down Collins Avenue on the way to a military hospital. I was so sick, I couldn't enjoy the trip, but I do remember the nice corporal behind the wheel. I appreciated the sympathetic look he gave me as he opened the door and said, "Tough luck, soldier." I looked around and took in my new environment and easily understood why it seemed so familiar-the Pancoast, with its look of the old South was a large old hotel that the government had converted into a hospital for guys like me.

I'll always rate the Pancoast Number Two among the bad hospital experiences I had while in the service. Of course, the Lazarett at Stalag V-A will remain Number One for all time.

CHAPTER 31

The Pancoast

At the Pancoast, I was placed in a ward with six beds. The orderlies, nurses, and doctors seemed entirely indifferent to our needs. The other men in my ward were sullen and uncommunicative, not even bothering to talk to one another. I learned that I was the only ex-prisoner of war among them, and a couple of my ward-mates acted as if they thought a P.O.W. was a traitor-someone who just threw up his hands and sat out the rest of the war. In later years, I discovered that even some of my friends felt that way.

When I tried to explain to my doctors the nature of my problems, they told me that was their job; they'd tell me what was wrong with me when they were good and ready. I remember that the doctor assigned to me had black hair and looked very young. He kept wiping his hair out of his eyes, which got on my nerves after a while. So, I told him he ought to get a GI-style crew cut, and he wouldn't have that problem any more. Somehow, I don't think he appreciated the subtle humor of my remark.

While in Pancoast, I took the first good look at my bald head since returning home. It didn't please me at all, but I was able to hang on to the attitude I'd begun to develop-that being bald and in this wretched hospital was sure a lot better than being belly-up in a grave in Europe. I consoled myself with the thought that God had made only a few perfect people, and put hair on everyone else. I also took comfort in my mother's homely wisdom, as I had done countless times overseas, and accepted my situation, as "Beshert," meant to be.

Only rarely did I see the same doctor twice. Most of them were interns, and I felt they were using me as a guinea pig. About three times a week, they would put me on a gurney and wheel me into a small room and subject me a painful proctoscopy, leaving me uncomfortable for hours to come. I kept asking for some results, but to hear the doctors talk, that must have been some kind of military secret. I would like to think these none-too-gentle ladies and gentlemen originated the expression, "up yours." Not even Kilroy would come to a place like this! And every day I demanded just a little more loudly than the time before that they send me home, a plea that seemed to fall on deaf ears.

What a relief it was to receive orders to proceed to the Welch Convalescent Hospital in glamorous Daytona Beach! This establishment reminded me more of a military post than a hospital, although the atmosphere felt much more relaxed than any other post I'd ever seen. The rooms were actually rather pleasant, still barracks-like, but not at all oppressive. Since we weren't confined to our beds, we had the run of the place. I certainly enjoyed roaming around, and made free use of all the facilities, including the Post Exchange. The doctors themselves were more relaxed too, and made an effort to explain to the patients what was going on, unlike the callous young doc I'd encountered at the Pancoast. Unfortunately, even here the doctors couldn't tell me much about my problems, except to say that they were a little more complicated than others', and that I needed to have patience.

At Welch, the administrators gave us two or three passes each week to visit town, and we could have weekend passes, too. Although a military-friendly city, Daytona Beach wasn't overcrowded, as was the case in other such places. I rarely saw rowdy, drunken servicemen, very unusual in comparison to other cities with bases nearby.

It took me just one week to realize that I wasn't going to get any better here. The doctors made their rounds once per day, made their notes, but offered me no treatment of any kind. I rode into the center of town almost every night and went to the movies.

One night, I took the bus with a couple of men who must have been in their thirties. After exiting, as the bus pulled away from us, a pickup truck with three gals in the cab stopped for the red light-two a little older and a younger one. My companions whistled at them and I yelled, "I'll take the one in the middle." The next thing we knew, they parked the truck, the one in the middle put her arm through mine, and we were paired up, just like that. We decided to go to a bar nearby where a trio was playing. I made do with club soda while everyone else guzzled real drinks of various descriptions.

I couldn't keep my eyes off my new friend, who was the spitting image-dimple and all-of Ava Gardner, the beautiful movie star. A couple of club sodas later we all went over to her house. As we were horsing around, the lights went out; a perfectly timed cue to start making out. The six of us did this for the next two nights, as well, but, on that third night, it occurred to me that these women were, "checking us out." I learned from my date that one of the other girls worked at the hospital and had looked up our records. She told me she knew that I had been a prisoner of war and that I was Jewish. She then told me she had been married to a Jewish soldier who'd been killed in action. As much as I liked her, and as easily as I could see myself getting involved, I surely didn't like the idea of her checking up on me. That was it! I never called her again.

Welch was a great hospital if there was nothing wrong with you. My problems, however-ceaseless gastrointestinal upset, stomach pains and hypertension-caused me great discomfort, to the point of my feeling all but completely overwhelmed when no treatment or improvement seemed forthcoming. I just wanted to go home. I requested a furlough, and to my amazement, I received a one-week leave immediately.

As soon as I arrived home, my mother took me off to a physician she knew, Dr. Leonard Birndorf. Once he understood my situation-that I had only a few days at home-he told me to report the next morning at six o'clock to Providence Hospital, where they ran me through a day-long series of tests. Dr. Birndorf called me later that evening and offered the first diagnosis of my condition that I'd heard to date: ulcerative colitis, hypertension, malnutrition, and frozen feet. This last was a symptom to which I had given no thought, was more severe than the others. Similarly, I had given no thought or notice to the pains in my back, neck and shoulders. Dr. Birndorf told me he'd be happy to recommend me for a medical discharge from the Army, and that I be placed in his care, "if I wished." Of course, I wished.

So, back to Welch Convalescent I went for a few hectic final days. I took my final regulation physical and dental examinations and requested my medical records so I could pass them on to Dr. Birndorf. The next steps in my separation from the Army took place in an office where I encountered the first female commissioned officer (other than a nurse) I'd ever met. I felt odd saluting her and almost called her, "Sir" when I offered the obligatory "Private First Class Brenner reporting..." After a brief but embarrassing pause, First Lieutenant Newbey cut in and returned my salute, saying simply, "Be seated, soldier."

She wore a khaki officer's uniform, of course with a skirt and the shiny silver bars of her rank on her epaulets. Her brown hair was cut short, and I detected no makeup on her face. She snapped pertinent questions and typed my answers on an Army form as fast as I could respond to them. She was very precise. She then handed me a manila envelope containing my records and explained in a military manner the code numbers on everything in the envelope. On top of the paperwork, I saw a blue pin for my uniform jacket signifying my discharge along with a lapel pin known lovingly in Army slang as the, "Ruptured Duck." Discharged soldiers wore this on their civilian clothes to indicate their status as veterans. Under my medical records, I found my official discharge papers, a railroad ticket back to Detroit-the city where I had been inducted-plus ration money. Lieutenant Newbey abruptly stood up, saluted me, and put out her hand. As we were shaking hands, she caught herself as she was about to say said, "Good luck, soldier," and said, "Good luck, civilian," instead.

I left the building and headed for the bus stop to get a ride into town. As I got on the bus, the driver noticed my blue pin. When I got off at the railroad station, he called out, "Good luck, soldier. Have a nice trip home." After calling my parents from a pay phone, I thought I might buy something a civilian could wear, but everything in the station shop was khaki. Now I pronounced two solemn vows: I would never starve again, and I would never more in my life wear anything khaki or brown!

Everything seemed to go well. Even the train was on time. For a change I found a good seat by the window. As the train pulled out, I remembered my first train trip to Camp Claiborne, Louisiana. For some reason, even though I was indescribably happy to be out of the service, I felt an empty lost feeling. I wondered what I would do now. I was on my way to a new life, and wouldn't have to march any more to anyone else's orders, or salute people I felt didn't deserve that kind of respect. I was conscious that a great transformation in my life had begun, and that the click-clack of the rails could only speed me on to bigger and better things.

I remembered the day I walked out of the prison camp, when several men swarmed to get to me to say goodbye and thank me for what I'd done men I didn't even recognize-they asked me my name and my hometown and wished me well. Some even wanted my autograph and home address. I certainly wouldn't have wanted them to see the tears welling up in my eyes, and that was the way I felt for all the rest of the train ride home.

Another thought that occupied my mind on the trip home, and in fact provided me with a great deal of comfort, had to do with my big idea for a career. For some time now, I'd known I wanted to become what used to be called a chiropodist (which profession is now called podiatry). While working in the Lazarett, I'd learned more about feet than most doctors would ever know, and I was sure I'd make a damned fine chiropodist. By now, that desire positively burned within me.

All in all, I felt pretty good, in spite of the wretched condition of the train car in which I rode. It smelled from the jam-packed crowds it had carried during the war, and the seats were musty and frayed. This car had surely seen better days. The well-dressed civilian sitting next to me acted every bit as beaten down as the worn-out rolling stock. He told me how he had suffered as a result of gasoline rationing and the different foods he couldn't buy, and especially the type of clothing he could no longer obtain because of the war. I couldn't resist telling this jerk that I didn't understand his unhappiness: I had just received two brand-new uniforms with no trouble at all! In fact, one was for summer and one for winter. I then told him it must be the clothes he was wearing that smelled so badly.

The stench from the old railroad car, coupled with the stink of the clothing worn by the man sitting next to me, now combined with the foul smell of the cigar he was smoking, overwhelming me to the point that I was literally gasping for breath. A shimmering haze seemed to engulf me, and the whole world suddenly looked to be the same color as his suit and cheap cigar: Shit-brindle brown.

CHAPTER 32

It's Tough To Be A Civilian

I began to feel uncomfortably warm-in fact I was sweating profusely, and the back of my khaki shirt was soaking wet. I felt myself immersed in a vision, almost as if my ghost was watching my physical self from a short distance away. Within an instant, the vision turned horribly ugly: I saw myself walking down the hall on the first floor of the Lazarett of Stalag 5A, just at the moment I had caught sight of the French Padre's body in the hands of a couple of tall, rough German soldiers. I saw the Padre fly across the hall and slam into the wall on the opposite side where he just sat there, not uttering one peep in pain. It seemed obvious to me that he'd dealt with these men before.

The Germans, in my vision, appeared very grand in their full-dress battle gear. They just looked at the pathetic figure on the floor and laughed. As one of them stepped aside, he pointed to me, indicating that I should walk into a long closet, whence emanated the terrible smell of the decaying corpse of an American soldier.

The corpse was lying on a litter next to the wall. The soldier pointed to the dog tags on a chain around the dead man's neck. With his other hand, he held out one finger and shouted, "einz" ("one"), which I understood to mean he wanted me to hand him one of the tags[1] The space in the closet was so confined that I had to force my feet under the edge of the stretcher as I removed the dog tag. These soldiers weren't any of the guards I knew; they had to have been combat troops who had brought the body over from the main hospital-the Kranenkhaus. As I struggled, to separate the tag from the chain they burst out laughing. Then, they slammed the closet door shut, locking me into that windowless tomb for three days and three horrifying nights.

Imagine this: Here I was on a train riding home to Detroit, but fully immersed in a ghastly true-to-life vision of an event that had occurred a few months before. My body reacted now just as it had back then-I vomited my guts up. Thank God a conductor shook me out of it. He was very understanding and helpful; perhaps he'd witnessed similar scenes before. He brought me some extra towels and toiletries for which I was grateful. I changed my shirt, and even though I was starting to feel better, I remained shaky for some time to come. When I got back to my seat I was greatly relieved to find my obnoxious seat mate gone. That compassionate conductor had put, "reserved" signs on both seats so I wouldn't have to sit next to anyone for the rest of the trip.

Little did I know then that this apparition of the corpse in the closet would be one of the four flashbacks I would experience on a regular basis for the rest of my life; whether as waking visions or nightmares. Little did I know that I was showing classic symptoms of Post-Traumatic Stress Disorder-a diagnosis that wouldn't exist (much less gain recognition by Veterans Administration authorities) until thirty years later!

---

1   Here the dream differed from the real-life experience. Whenever a man died in the Lazarett, one of his dog tags would remain with the corpse, and I would take the other. I would then pass the one in my possession through to the camp authorities, who would send it to the International Red Cross, who would send it on to U.S. military authorities. In this particular case I ended up keeping the dog tag and forgetting about it, and only tried to send it on to the man's family after I returned to the United States.

I tried to relax by closing my eyes and thinking about how it used to be at home. Among the many memories flooding into my mind right then, I recalled my father nailing an old orange or apple crate outside the kitchen window to hold our perishable foods during the winter months-our fresh-air refrigerator. I used to get a big kick from taking the frozen milk bottle out of the window box. It was so cold, the cream rose to the top and pushed the cap in the bottle up, with the cream sticking out between the bottle and the cap.

I also remembered that my mother baked challah-the special braided egg-bread we ate on the Sabbath-and made noodles for the chicken soup. She did this even on days she wasn't feeling well. She just had to do her own baking and not buy anything ready-made. Rather than watch her struggle, I told her I'd go out to the store and buy what we needed, and then she'd always come out with her favorite expressions: "Where there's a will there's a way." "You learn something every day." "You need to crawl before you can walk." "If there's a job to be done, do it well, or not at all." Her simple philosophy exerted a great influence on my life, then as well as later.

We pulled into a railroad station in one of the small towns of the South. I noticed many small cars lined up at the curb by the station entrance. This scene brought back a memory of one of my brother, Saul's old cars, an REO Coupe-a two-seater with a stick shift. In my mind's eye, I saw it parked in front of our house. I must have been about ten years old at the time. Saul was asleep, and I decided to take his keys and move the car about ten feet up from its present position. Before I knew it, I had passed about five cars and thought I'd better back up. Unfortunately, I couldn't work the gearshift well enough to find reverse gear, so I had to continue forward. Luckily, I was able to park up ahead at the next corner. I ran back to the house and stealthily put the keys back where I'd found them. About an hour later, Saul had to go somewhere and when he couldn't find his car, he was just about to call the police. At that point, I thought the better of it and confessed. He just laughed. Hurrying through the door, he called back, "The next time you want to drive, take me with you!"

Now that the war with Japan had ended, my brother, Myer had enough service points to be among the first group to earn his discharge. Thinking of him as I rode the train home from Florida, I found myself once again becoming agitated, as emotions of all kinds seemed to wash over me. I could hardly wait to see him. I realized that even though he had spent the entire war overseas and had been in combat most of the time, he still sought and found opportunities to write to me, even after I was declared missing and all of his letters were returned home marked as such. Myer was six years older than I, we had our sibling rivalries. He'd always given me a hard time when we were kids, but now I realized he loved me and was concerned for my well-being.

At the end of the long and challenging train trip, my homecoming started out on a frustrating note. I was a total rookie in the civilian game: I felt completely lost in the civilian world and couldn't seem to find anything I needed to get my life going again, especially clothing. I combed the shops of Detroit for three full weeks in search of something that would fit my short and skinny frame, but between my odd size and the ongoing shortage of consumer goods, I struck out over and over again. I finally found a suit at Richman Brothers, an inexpensive chain store. It was navy blue with a white chalk stripe-the kind of outfit a small-time gangster might wear!

I was still very sick from malnutrition, diarrhea, and ulcerative colitis. At the age of twenty-three, I was supposed to be experiencing the prime of my life, but like so many young men who went to war, I felt like a lost soul; happy though I was to have left the service. I had a lot of time on my hands to think, and I spent a lot of nights wishing I could drift off to sleep. Sleep, however, appeared to be out of the question, as I couldn't help but relive the long, sleepless nights in Stalag 5A. If I did happen to doze off, my relentless nightmares soon jolted me awake. At night, even in the comfort and security of my family home, I felt as if I were back in the camp, submerged in enforced darkness. There, we had no lights we could switch on; my five bunk mates and I lay in our tiny eight-by-ten room with our six wooden racks stacked three-high on each side of the wall. I had the lower bunk by the door in case I had to get up to receive wounded men during the night. We talked hour after hour during those nights about food and our favorite restaurants. The married men wondered if their wives knew they were still alive. None of us got any mail. Most nights, the conversation would arrive at a point where all six of us were crying about how much we loved our wives and girlfriends. I was the only one without a special girl, but I cried along with them. Every night, we took an oath that we'd never starve again.

Always on my mind during those long hours of darkness in the camp were thoughts of my parents. Did they know I was alive? Had I ever told them I loved them? The nights in the prison camp actually became precious to me as I realized what a wonderful family I had and how special was my past. It took the rigors of combat, capture, captivity and homecoming to make me understand this: better late than never!

The physical ills I'd picked up as a prisoner of war stayed with me a long time.

CHAPTER 33

A Serviceman's Readjustment Acts: Part 2

Sick as I was, I wanted very much to get on with my life, which, right that minute, meant going to school and earning the degree, I needed to become a practicing chiropodist. I applied to a school in Cleveland, only to learn that I needed to pick up several liberal arts credits before they'd admit me. So, I enrolled in the Detroit Institute of Technology's evening program, taking courses in speech, criminology, and one other subject.

I struggled for three months, finally realizing that my body as well as my mind was simply not up to the task. The ulcerative colitis would not ease up. Even more troubling, my nerves just couldn't take the pressure, of the schoolwork or anything else, for that matter. In no uncertain terms, Dr. Birndorf told me, "Go somewhere, anywhere. Get out of town. Forget about school. Have a good time, or you'll end up with a nervous breakdown."

How lucky I was to run into my old school chum, Hy Shannon, who was about to take off for California. He needed someone to drive out there with him, which sounded pretty good to me. He was ready to go at that very moment, but I asked him if he could wait a day; if so, I'd pack up what I needed and join him. He agreed, and next thing I knew, we were on the road to the West Coast. I was feeling better by the minute! While not exactly relaxing, our road trip was uneventful and enjoyable all the way.

Thanks to one more stroke of good fortune, I encountered another of my friends from Detroit who was vacationing in Los Angeles. I shared a room with him for a month, and then took a short jaunt up to San Francisco, where I spent a most pleasant weekend with my sister, Fanny. By this time, I wanted to relocate permanently to California, but I felt I needed to get myself home to Detroit before too much more time passed, and move on with rebuilding my life. California would have to wait. So, I hopped on a Greyhound bus (it took about five days to cover the distance) and found myself again in the midst of my wonderful family.

I hadn't been home long when, much to my surprise, I received a visit from two F.B.I. agents. After they'd made sure that I was indeed the Samuel Seymour Brenner for whom they were looking, they told me in no uncertain terms that I was never to speak of my experience as a prisoner of war to anyone, not even my family. Nor was I to write about it, speak in public, or publish anything that even referred to my time as a, "guest" of the Germans, as some of my fellow kriegies liked to put it. An outstanding feature of this meeting remains clear as day in my memory: One of the agents kept going to our living room window, parting the curtains and peering outside. When I asked him what he was looking for, he said, "This isn't such a great neighborhood. I just want to make sure nobody steals our car!" F.B.I. agents visited me two more times during the next couple of years to remind me of the rules. Although I was more scared of them than anything else, in a strange way, I suppose they made me feel I was a bit of a special case after all. They also asked me if I recognized a couple of names; I told them I didn't, and I didn't engage them on the subject any further at the time. It only occurred to me years later that these might have been the names of men I had treated in the Lazarett, maybe even Whitey, whose leg I had helped to amputate, or the other guy whose toe I had lopped off with a pair of shears. In the late 1990s (only fifty years later!), I actually called the F.B.I. office in Detroit to see if any record existed of this meeting, and, if perhaps I could learn anything more of those names. But, the agent with whom I spoke told me all records of that period had been destroyed back in 1954.

I wonder if anyone ever got so much enjoyment from his, "52-20 Club" money as I did. This was the unemployment insurance that the GI Bill provided; twenty dollars per week for a year. That might not sound like much, but it was enough to get by in reasonable comfort. I knew it wouldn't last forever, so I tried again to buckle down and get a job, even though Dr. Birndorf had reaffirmed his advice that I should avoid stress. I had a chance to go to Chicago and work on some radio shows, but not wanting to leave home again quite then, I turned it down. I did, however, finally begin to put my knowledge of feet to good use, although not in any way I'd previously anticipated: I took a job in a shoe store, selling shoes.

One day, while taking my lunch break at a barbecue restaurant near the store, I caught sight of six good-looking girls jammed into a booth on the other side of the room, obviously having a good time. Since I knew one of them, I walked over and tried to meet the others, successfully, as it turned out. One of the young ladies, named Resa, even gave me her phone number. As soon as I got home from work, I called her. When she picked up the receiver, I said, "Hi Resa, this is Sy!" "Who?" She retorted, rather plaintively. "The guy you met in the restaurant just a little while ago!" And that was the start of a beautiful romance; we got married a year later. I guess it was "Beshert"!

I found a much better job with a record distributor, travelling from Michigan to Ohio trying to convince radio disk jockeys and jukebox owners to play our company's records. The business boomed between 1949 and 1950, but began to slow down as television found its way into more and more homes. Resa's sister was living in California then, so we decided to move out there. I was still under Dr. Birndorf's care, but he told me he thought I'd be all right if I were careful, took all my medicines, and found another physician who was experienced in the kinds of problems I'd been having. So, off we went.

Right away, I found work as a milkman, delivering dairy products to homes in a couple of Los Angeles neighborhoods. The hours seemed ideal to me: four o'clock in the morning until noon, which meant I could spend the rest of the day looking for a real job. On my rounds one day I met a Fuller Brush Man, who told me I could make good money doing what he did. So, I kept my milkman's job in the mornings and sold Fuller Brush products door to door in the afternoons. During a collection call at a customer's home, the man of the house told me a smart salesman like me could do even better selling his company's TV sets. So I put a booklet together with pictures of the available models and their prices and carried that with me, and was soon selling three televisions a week, all while doing my other two jobs!

Resa's uncle, who owned a children's store in Los Angeles, gave me the idea that would finally turn into a lifetime career, to go to work as a clothing manufacturer's representative. I got off to a good start, and within three months had a line of my own to sell-Chic Tots. My territory included California, Arizona and Nevada. By 1960, my success earned me a much more prestigious line to sell-Cinderella Dresses-the largest and most highly advertised dress firm in the world.

It occurred to me that by creating an educational program about my product to present to elementary and junior high school classes, I might be able to stimulate some real demand for Cinderella dresses. From the factory, I obtained photos and other documentary materials that I used to tell the story of how dresses were made and marketed. My presentation began in the fields where the fiber crops were grown, moved to the design stage, then to the workshops where cutters and seamstresses assembled the dresses, and ended in the retail store. I made this into a slide show that I took to schools throughout my territory, and it worked even better that I had hoped. Students and teachers alike loved it, and when the children's parents took them shopping for clothes, the girls almost inevitably asked for Cinderella dresses. My name and program appeared in school system resource books, articles were written about me in trade journals, and I even made the cover of a national magazine as the subject of an article entitled, "Smart Salesman Goes to School."

I became head of the Los Angeles office and had a whole corps of salesmen working for me. I had characters on popular television shows such as, "Family Affair" wearing our products on screen and strutting them at fashion shows. I put on seminars for department stores, and their advertising departments. Clearly, I was loving my work and doing very well at it. This was the story of my life for the next twenty-five years, until, suddenly, something appeared to have changed.

What was wrong with this picture? I had a lovely wife, three smart, funny grown children, a home in Beverly Hills, and a most enviable record with my company. Why then, did my colleagues ask me one day to stop talking with our accounts? It seems I had become rather rude and abrasive; at least, that's what those who were closest to me were now saying. They told me something was wrong with my jokes, which were now offending and even frightening people. This assertion couldn't have shocked me more, given that my sense of humor had earned quite a glowing reputation over the years. I had always enjoyed offering jokes, humorous stories, nonsensical poems, and songs in moments when I thought they were appropriate. Now, I learned that coworkers, friends, and our customers, found me obnoxious. Something about me had changed, and I couldn't figure out what it was.

Fortunately, I had enough good sense to take stock of the situation and ponder what I might do about it. Laid low one day by a bout of bronchitis, I stayed home from work, and it came to me that I had been feeling lately as if I were under a great deal of stress of the same kind and quality I had experienced many years before. I called Resa and my daughter at my office (both were working for me at the time) and told them I was going to retire A.S.A.P.. We would sell the house and move to San Diego.

While they could understand the pressure that the business placed on me, my family had no idea whatsoever that I had struggled with such stress for a long time, in fact, since the war. Given that I had never and I mean never-discussed with them what I'd done or what happened to me during the war, their ready acceptance of my condition now was all the more remarkable. They stood by me as I resigned from Cinderella, sold the house, moved to San Diego, and took up a completely different way of life. All this took place in 1986.

We hadn't been in San Diego long, when I saw a fellow named Mel Madero appear on a local television program, talking about the relationship between the prisoner of war experience and Post-Traumatic Stress Disorder (P.T.S.D.). Madero was commander of the San Diego chapter of a national organization called American Ex-Prisoners of War, or AX-P.O.W.'s for short. He said that most ex-P.O.W.'s probably suffered from this ailment, and that the V.A. was better equipped than ever before to help veterans deal with it. Madero mentioned that his group of former prisoners met every week at the Veterans Administration center in San Diego's Mission Valley, and he extended an invitation to any ex-P.O.W.'s in the viewing audience to give him a call with any questions they might have, or better yet, to drop in at a weekly meeting.

I called him right away, and, instantly a whole new world opened up to me. I learned that many of the issues that had plagued me for the past forty-plus years-my recurring nightmares, my irritability, abrasiveness, nervousness, "hyper-vigilance", and reticence about my wartime experiences were likely all symptoms of P.T.S.D.. I learned as well that the psychological and medical professions had only recently (1980) accepted P.T.S.D. as a real-life diagnosis and incorporated it in the third edition of the Diagnostic and Statistical Manual, the bible of American psychology and psychiatry. Finally, I learned that AX-P.O.W.'s had been instrumental in gaining the attention of the United States Congress, which even then was in process of passing legislation mandating recognition, benefits and treatment by the Veterans Administration for former P.O.W.'s, which had not been available until this very moment.

Joining the group provided me with as near a, "born-again" experience as I'll ever have. I met fifty or more men, all of whom knew exactly what I'd been through during the war. I was amazed to hear stories from former soldiers, sailors, marines and aviators, some of whom had suffered much more hardship that I could even imagine possible. This was especially the case with those who had been captured in the Pacific Theater of Operations; for all the privation I'd gone through, the Japanese treated their prisoners much more harshly than had the Germans. Among the closest friends I made in this group were Al McGrew and Leon Beck, both captured in the Philippines early in the war. Beck started out on the infamously cruel Bataan Death March, managed to escape, and fought in the jungle as a guerrilla with Filipino Rangers for most of the next three years, until American forces recaptured the islands. McGrew was taken prisoner on Corregidor, which fell about a month after Bataan. He spent the rest of the war in prison camps in the Philippines and later in Japan, where he suffered some of the very worst that mankind had to offer, including frequent beatings, near-starvation, and slave labor. And I thought I'd had it tough!

Above: Sy Brenner and Jack Roland

All of us ex-P.O.W.'s now found common cause serving each other. The group's leaders fought tirelessly on several fronts to improve our lot in life. They challenged our representatives in Congress to continue to recognize and fulfill our needs; they challenged the practitioners in the health care branch of the V.A. to investigate and treat our physical and psychological maladies; and they performed feats of heroism with the V.A.'s benefits branch to ensure we received the disability ratings, family services, pensions and other payments we'd been denied for so long. And they never let up with their outreach program to locate and enroll "forgotten" ex-P.O.W.'s such as I, who had never known that such relief was even available.

Upon joining the group, I was assigned a social worker who led me through the process of signing up for assessments and evaluations I would need to qualify for treatments and benefits. Among other discoveries, I found out that my jokes were still coming out wrong-a sure sign that my head needed further shrinking, if you know what I mean! One of my new comrades, Jack Roland, a paratrooper captured in Europe a little later in the war than I had been, researched my service records and had all my medals and citations restored to me, including the Purple Heart, Bronze Star and P.O.W. Medal.

The Director of Chaplain services at the V.A. Medical Services, who was a regular attendee and important contributor to the P.O.W. group meetings, introduced me to another V.A. Chaplain, the Reverend Bill Mahedy. At that moment, I was preparing a short talk that was to be part of the dedication ceremony for our AX-P.O.W. chapter's incoming Commander, Charlie Miller. Miller had been at the controls of a B-17 Flying Fortress when he was shot down over Europe. His P.O.W. experience included no fewer than seven escapes from prison camps, which had earned him the reputation as a real troublemaker and, "hard case" for his captors. Mahedy and Miller had become especially close friends, and I found it an honor and a privilege to join this little circle.

Bill Mahedy had been a Catholic Priest, and had served as an Army Chaplain in combat in Vietnam. Later, however, he left the Catholic Church, took new holy orders as an Episcopalian Priest, married and raised a family. During the mid-1970s and thereafter, he became an outspoken advocate for the Vietnam veterans movement, and was instrumental guiding the V.A. to recognize P.T.S.D.. In San Diego, Mahedy-by now a renowned authority on P.T.S.D., founded the first Vet Center, a storefront outpatient and veterans' services office where troubled vets could find a less bureaucratic and more welcoming environment than they might encounter at a main V.A. Hospital. Here Mahedy led "rap sessions," providing group and individual therapy to hundreds of veterans who might not otherwise seek or obtain any help from the V.A..

"Love at first sight" is the only way I can describe my introduction to Bill Mahedy. He took me to lunch, during which we spent the entire time telling jokes to each other and singing the kind of nonsense songs that had been so much a feature of my earlier life. Needless to say, we became very great friends. For most of the next two years, Bill provided me with the best psychological and spiritual therapy I had ever received. He managed to get right to the heart of my troubles with post-traumatic stress. Ever since then, I've referred to him as "my Episcopalian Rabbi." In fact, Bill was the only one outside of my immediate family invited to my eight-fifth birthday celebration-that's how close we remain.

When a few years later, my regular V.A. Physician sent me to a V.A. Psychiatrist, I learned just how expert and how effective Bill Mahedy's therapy had been. The new doctor asked me the same questions Mahedy had: When you look out of a window, do you peek out from the corner, or focus from the center? When you walk on a sidewalk, do you look out ahead, or down at the pavement? Bill had already told me that because I looked out from the corner of windows, I was still on the watch for snipers, and that when I looked down at the sidewalk, I was searching for land mines. Before long, the doc told me that Bill was better at this game than he'd ever be.

Thanks to people such as Bill Mahedy and my new cohort's of ex-P.O.W. comrades, I found myself ready as never before to tell my story; something that I could now do because I could trust the sympathy and empathy of my fellows. They'd been there, and they'd know what I was talking about. I started appearing before classes of students of all ages and at military ceremonies, even leading groups on tours at the Museum of Tolerance in Los Angeles. And I've been active with the EX-P.O.W. group ever since, slowing down and cutting back my participation only after Resa and I moved into an assisted-living home that couldn't always provide transportation to the Thursday meetings. I'm still being treated for P.T.S.D., and I still seek every opportunity to talk with students of all ages about what happened in my life. And even though the end of our captivity occurred more than sixty years ago, the group is still bringing in new members!

DEPARTMENT OF VETERANS AFFAIRS
San Diego Healthcare System
3350 La Jolla Village Drive
San Diego CA 92161

Nov. 30, 2000

To Whom It May Concern:

This is to confirm that Mr. Samuel (Sy) Brenner served in the army during WWII. He was wounded in action and taken prisoner by the Germans and held until the end of the war. During this period Mr. Brenner suffered hardships and stressful situations that are beyond the range of normal human experience. He was a combat medic and, when captured, was placed by his captors in charge of medical treatment for prisoners. These experiences have embedded themselves deeply upon his memory. He is now able to speak quite openly and effectively about his time in captivity.

Mr. Brenner has been a member of the VA San Diego ex-POW support group. He is a very active member, attending almost every meeting. He has also participated in a University of California, San Diego class taught by Dr. Abraham Schragge. He has spoken to members of this class and held them in rapt attention. He has spoken to other groups of students, has participated in displays of POW memorabilia, has granted interviews to students who have used his experiences as a basis for class papers and he has contributed in major ways to the advancement of the POW cause in San Diego.

I have seen parts of Mr. Brenner's manuscript which recounts his experiences during WWII and their enduring effects. His story is among the most fascinating accounts I have ever heard or read. This veteran is highly effective, articulate, sensitive person. In fact, he is remarkable by any standards.

Anything that can be done to assist him in making known his story would be most beneficial, not just for him, but for anyone who might read what he has written. Mr. Brenner, besides being a magnificent human being, is an outstanding example of the resilience of the human spirit.

Sincerely,

William P. Mahedy
Chaplain, Posttraumatic Stress Clinical Team

William "Bill" Mahedy's letter

SY BRENNER
Popular speaker — then and now

● **Sy Brenner** has been honored with an invitation to address the graduation ceremony of the Naval School of Health Services on Sept. 12. Brenner began speaking at schools and other organization during the Gulf War, relating some of his experiences as a nazi-held Jewish POW during World War II. He also has spoken to **Dr. Abe Schragge**'s classes at UCSD on "War and Prisoners of War" over the past eight years. In addition to his many speaking engagements, Brenner, through Jewish Family Service, has escorted busloads of high school seniors to the **Museum of Tolerance** in Los Angeles.

All of us ex-P.O.W.'s now found common cause serving each other. We challenged congress to continue to recognize and fulfill our needs.

CHAPTER 34

Being Honored

In 1995, a ceremony was held at the Capitol Rotunda in Washington, D.C. honoring all the infantry Divisions who liberated concentration camps. I knew nothing about the 103rd Infantry Division being involved in the liberation, because I was being held as a P.O.W., until my wife and I received an invitation to this ceremony.

Our cousin, Mel Wachs, picked up Resa and me a few days before the ceremony. Mel showed us around Washington, D.C.. On the day of the ceremony, he drove us right up to the Capitol steps where spikes that came up in the street, and was approached by two guards with dogs stopped him. They searched the car and the dogs sniffed out the trunk.

Mel worked for the government and had high-level security clearance, so we watched as the spikes in the road were lowered, and Mel was able to drive us right to the elevator that took us and two guards who were escorting us, directly the Capitol Rotunda.

As we got off the elevator and walked into the Rotunda, we saw thousands of vets sitting there with flags representing their individual infantry Divisions.

I was wearing my Army hat, which had a large cactus on it. A man way on the other side of the room yelled, "Hey, 103rd Division, over here". He pointed to two chairs right behind him. After we introduced ourselves, this man from Texas told us he had written a book about the 103rd Division. He told us where we could go find our records about the 103rd Division, and day-by-day records of what happened to our regiment while in combat.

Following our discussion, the ceremony began with Benjamin Mead, a Holocaust survivor, who organized the event. After, there were speeches by congressmen and notable senators. When the ceremony was over, we walked out to the nearest corner, and were wondering where to spend the rest of the afternoon. We saw a gentleman walking toward us and asked him where the nearest museum was. He was carrying a very old, peeling leather briefcase, and he said in a very heavy Russian accent, "Air and Space Museum", and he pointed to the museum. First, he told us to take a taxi, then he said, "Vait, I take you in my car." A limo pulled up to the curb, and he opened the back door and motioned us to get in. He sat in the front and told the driver where to take us. My wife asked him about his family, and I asked him where he was from. He said, "I Ambassador from Lithuania". When we pulled up to the museum, he got out and opened the door for us. As we got out of the car, he yelled at his driver, "take me get hot dog". We couldn't help but laugh.

The next day, we went to the Holocaust Museum. The following day, we went to the National Archives to see the records of the 410th Infantry Regiment. We had been told to take a roll of quarters, since every page we wanted to copy cost a quarter. The records were brought out on a large library cart. That is where found out how I was hit, and where I was taken prisoner. The place was Nothalden, France. The records were taken to a desk and inspected. The ones that I could have declassified were given to me, and the others were withheld. I looked at records while Mel made the copies.

This is also when I learned that on the night of November 29, 1944, seven medics in our outfit were killed, wounded, or taken prisoner.

I never forgot the brief but intense friendship I'd developed with Pol and Zaig Monjarret during my last weeks in the prison camp. After the war, they sent me a wooden box that Pol had carved himself, which since then has always had a place of honor on my coffee table-a fond reminder of one of the few good experiences I'd had during the war.

CHAPTER 35

Epilogue

BODADEG AR SONERION
(Assemblée des Sonneurs)

Pol MONJARRET
41, Rue Notre-Dame
GUINGAMP
(Côtes-du-Nord)

le 20 janvier 1946

my dear Sam,

I was very happy to receive any news from you. Following which Louizaig has just said you. I have not many things to add. But I must thank you very much of your proposition to send us packages. Here we lack everything we are cold, we are hungry, but spirits is good still because spring is approaching.

I will send you souvenirs from Brittany.

I will develop the photos made on the day of our liberation at Ludwigsburg and shall send them to you. Some are not very beautiful, but it will be at least a souvenir.

It is a great dommage you could not have entered with us France in our small car, we entered Paris four days later; we passed with our guns for hunting, cameras, etc...

Happily American soldiers gave us gazoline.

an american cannot fancy the life we have in France nowadays. The shops are empty. The Jerries have taken every things before starting - It does not go better - a worker hardly can live with his pay - we hope better days.

Surely we will go and see you to Detroit, if, one day we have an occasion to go to America, and I hope you will come to Brittany if you come to France. This is our new address.

Louizaig and Pol Monjarret
42 Rue Notre-Dame
Guingamp (Côtes du Nord)
France (Bretagne)

Thank for us your brothers and sisters. who are very kind to help you for sending us packages.

I end for to-day

Sincerely yours

Monjarret

P.S. Do you know a young boy who should be glad to correspond with my brother Anthony - he collects stamps and should like to have a friend in America to change stamps with him.

Above: Letter from Pol and Zaig

On a warm, sleepy summer afternoon-July 25, 1994, to be precise-I wa relaxing at home in the room I called my office. As I sat in my comfortable swive chair, I glanced through the open door of the closet, and noticed an old box wher I kept pictures and letters dating back to before the war. I felt suddenly draw to it, as if by a mysterious electromagnetic force. It had been some time since I' peeked inside this box, but now, unable to resist, I removed the top, pulled out packet of papers and untied the worn blue ribbon holding it together. My min suddenly flooded with vivid memories of events both wonderful and horrific tha had occurred fifty years earlier. I cleared a space on my desk and spread out som items I hadn't seen for a long time-the contents of a yellowing envelope addresse to me in an obviously foreign hand, with French stamps affixed in the upper, righ hand corner. Now, on the desk before me, I beheld photos and letters from Po and Zaig Monjarret, the French couple I had met quite by accident late one nigh in the spring of 1945, when, as a prisoner of war, I was returning from one of m clandestine meetings with The Lady.

I had begun to receive mail from the Monjarrets when I'd been in the hospita during the summer of 1945. Their letters filled me with a combination of sadnes and guilt because the war had so completely impoverished them. Not long after th Monjarrets had married, the Germans destroyed their farm and laid waste to all th area around them. Upon their return home after liberation, it had proven extremel difficult for them even to begin to rebuild their lives. When I communicated thi nformation to my family, my sisters, Clara and Rae and my sister-in-law, Helen resolved with me to do everything we could to help these distant friends. Just about every other week, for the next few years, we sent Pol and Zaig, "care packages" with everything we imagined they'd need to keep themselves going or enjoy-canned and dried foods, candy, clothing, and especially cigarettes, which were more valuable than French currency at the time. International postal rules dictated that our packages weigh no more than eleven pounds, and we carefully made sure to fill our parcels to the maximum and not one ounce more.

As I read one of the letters, a pang of regret swept through me, for I'd lost contact with the Monjarrets after I'd moved to California in 1950. Now, yet another strange sensation overtook me, something that had never occurred to me until just this moment. Out of the blue, I wanted to return to Europe and face the ordeal I had experienced in the prison camp. Not five minutes passed before I found myself embarked on a search for Pol and Zaig. My first step was writing to the mayor of Guingamp, the Monjarret's hometown in the French department of Brittany.

One thing led to another in remarkably short order. In less than two weeks' time, I found a telephone message from Paris awaiting me on my answering machine. Catherine Monjarret, Pol and Zaig's niece, had called to tell me that the mayor of Guingamp had sent her my letter, because he knew she could read and understand English. She said in her taped message she had heard about me throughout her life, and was so excited, she had to call me right away. She went on to say she had forwarded my letter to her aunt

Samuel Brenner
6429 Gem Lake Avenue
San Diego, California 92119 U.S.A.
Telephone (619) 464-1244

Maire De Guingamp 33-96 406 440
22200 C. D'Armor
Bretagne, France

July 25, 1994

Dear Maire,

My name is Sam Brenner. I was a prisoner of war in Germany, Stalag VA near Ludwigsberg.

I am trying to locate a couple from Guingamp that I met when the war was near its end. They are Mr. and Mrs. Pol Monjarret. At that time they lived at 42 Rue Notre - Dame.

After the war I sent them parcels and Pol was nice enough to make a hand carved box for me. At this time, I lived in Detroit, Michigan U.S.A.

After I got married, I moved to California in 1950. I lost contact with Pol and his wife at this time. I think of them often and recall all of the very hard times that they had.

In recent years I have had a very strong desire to return to France. I was wounded and taken prisoner in Southern France. I would like to also return to Ludwigsberg to see where I was as a prisoner.

My desire is to make this trip some time next Spring. I would like to find Pol and his lovely wife before then so I could arrange to see them when I am there. I think of them and look at their pictures often.

If you could have them, or any family members, contact me or send me any information you can find, I would appreciate it very much.

Please note my name, address, and telephone number at the top of this letter.

Sincerely,

Sam (Sy) Brenner

Above: Sy Brenner is looking for Pol and Zaig

and uncle; at that point the message tape ended, without her having left me a return number. I called directory assistance in Paris, but to no avail. Apparently, she had an unlisted phone.

A few days later, while my Detroit, cousins, Milton and Zelda Rose were visiting we were talking about my experiences with Pol and Zaig when the phone rang. Imagine my surprise and the look on Milt's face when I heard the voice on the other end of the line saying, "This is Polig!" Having received my letter, he called as soon as he could, from Plomeur in Brittany. He was crying, and then I started to cry. Pol said, "Sam, I am an old man now." I asked him how old he was, and he told me he'd turned seventy-four. I laughed and replied that at seventy-three, I was an old man, too.

I was so delighted by this turn of events that I completely forgot that when we'd first met, Pol didn't speak a word of English; Zaig did all the talking and wrote the letters. He explained to me now that he had received a very liberal and practical education after the war. He'd been elected mayor of his town, and that job had required extensive international travel. Moreover, he'd become an author and composer. Before hanging up, Pol said he would follow up with a detailed letter about his life and family. The next day, Zaig called, saying she didn't want to get cheated out of talking to me.

A week or so later, I received not only a long letter from Pol, in French, which I had to get translated, but a thick package containing a heavy book written in English: author, Polig Monjarret. In it, he related the destiny of Breton culture and the folk music of the region. From this, I learned that bagpipes were native to Brittany, and that the Breton people felt more kinship with the Irish and Welsh than with the French. This last detail led to a discussion of Breton separatism and nationalism. It turns out that Pol himself was a leader in a separatist movement-an affiliation that cost him six months in a French prison. In the package with Pol's book, was one of the most beautiful magazines I'd ever seen, called Armen. Included in its pages was a large section about Pol with many photographs of him, past as well as present. I knew that he and Zaig were no country bumpkins, but his postwar education and sophistication surprised me. In return for his generous gift, I sent him some videotapes of television programs on which I'd appeared, talking about my P.O.W. experience.

We spoke several times after that, always concluding with expressions of our desire to meet again soon. After hanging up on one occasion, one of Pol and Zaig's daughters immediately called back and asked if, when we came to France, she might join her parents, because she felt as if she'd known me all her life. That was all it took; I began to plan the trip in earnest. After setting up a reunion with the Monjarrets, my second priority was to revisit all the places I had walked fifty years earlier as a member of the 103rd Infantry Division. Naturally, I wanted to see the prison hospital where I'd been in charge of the surgery section.

All I remembered of the place where I was taken prisoner, was a blown-up farm house in the village of Nothalden, but I didn't recall at all its specific location. So, I put on my detective hat and managed to establish contact with a travel agent in Michigan who had arranged a reunion for the 103rd Division. He told me to call a man named Richard Pearson in Piqua, Ohio, who had the 2nd Battalion records for the 410th Regiment. The trail was getting warm! I called Mr. Pearson, who proved to be very friendly and cooperative. When I gave him my name, rank and serial number, he found me right on his roster, with the notation "K.I.A. (killed in action) 29 November 1944 at Nothalden, France." Then, I heard a loud "Huh!" When Mr. Pearson accepted that he wasn't, in fact, talking with a ghost, we resumed our conversation as any two live guys would.

Mr. Pearson told me about the many reunions I'd missed, and he offered a lot of suggestions about places I should see and people with whom I should speak. My niece, Cindy Newman, who is a travel agent, began to put the whole pilgrimage together, down to the minute details of how long it would take us to drive from one town to another, including some that weren't even on the map any more. We had a remarkable stroke of luck when one of the agents in Cindy's office heard we wanted to go to the out-of-the way city of Ludwigsburg, Germany-a place not visited by many American tourists. It so happened that Cindy's colleague had a friend who had just returned from there-a twenty-seven year old student named Tom Voight, whose mother lived in Seeheim, a suburb of Ludwigsburg. Tom, who was visiting at the time in San Diego, was writing a paper on tourism. We met this young man several times, and he indicated he'd be willing to try to locate the prison camp and hospital building, enlisting his mother's help if necessary. He actually obtained this information for us in the form of a letter from the mayor of Ludwigsburg with a color map of the city that had the camp and hospital clearly marked.

Our further preparations fell into place nearly as well. My wife's sister and brother-in-law, Lois and Morey Sein, would accompany us, and we'd leave on my birthday, June 2, 1995. Two weeks prior to our departure, I sent a letter to the mayor of St. Die.

I was a little disappointed that I didn't hear back from him, but then another near-miracle occurred. Having just passed through security at San Diego airport on June 2, I heard my name called out over the airport paging system. The operator said that I had a very important phone call from France. I called my daughter, Mo at her home and learned that she had just taken a call from Françoise Brintais, the assistant to the mayor of St. Die. The mayor wanted us to call in advance of our arrival so we could meet some of the people who were there during World War II. It was at this moment that the excitement of the trip really set in as never before. We were on our way.

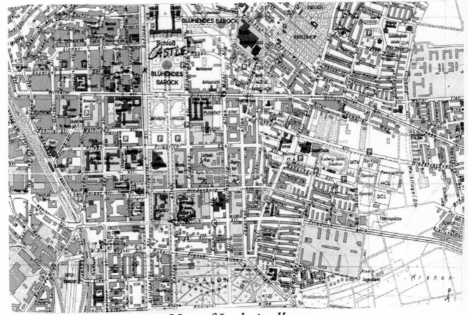

Map of Ludwigsdburg

We stopped in London for a day and a half, and from there, flew on to Strasbourg arriving late at night. I got up early the next morning to enjoy the beautiful city It turned out to be a holiday that day, and thousands of people from France and Germany jammed the streets. The stores were closed, and so was the car renta agency. We took a boat tour of the lovely canals that ran through the old par of town, feasting our eyes on the three-hundred year old homes. We wanted to visit the old cathedral, but the lines were too long. After lunch, we found that the English language tours of the museums weren't scheduled to start for two more hours, so we decided to head back to the hotel. It had started to rain quite hard but we couldn't find a taxi; we ended up walking back drenched. I had suffered two strokes in recent years (one occurred in the midst of, and perhaps because of, the nightmare I was having at the time-of the rats crawling over my face while I wa sleeping on the floor of the old stable), and these were clearly taking their toll on me: I was all but exhausted when we returned to the hotel. I knew I was going to have to pace myself if we were going to accomplish our goals. I hoped Lois, More' and Resa would be willing to bear with me.

Back in our room, I found a message awaiting me from Françoise Brintais. returned her call and told her we would try to be in St. Die the following afternoon I also called Tom Voight's mother in Seeheim, telling her when we thought we'c get to Ludwigsburg. She said she'd find us a hotel and reserve rooms for us. Nex morning, we picked up our comfortable rental car, and with Morey at the wheel off we went.

Our drive through the Vosges Mountains was breathtakingly beautiful. appreciated it now in a manner I could not have done fifty years earlier. We had great fun along the way; stopping at a picturesque old French inn that looked a if the Three Musketeers might come walking out the door. We had onion soup for lunch that was much better than the onion soup I'd eaten in Marseilles a long time ago. As we continued on the road to St. Die, I began to feel some twinges of apprehension; a sense of trauma was definitely building within me.

The town of St. Die-the largest in the region, with a population of 23,000-stands out in my memory for several reasons. Images of the battle we fought there, one of the biggest I remember, flooded into my consciousness. (In fact, postwar histories state that the battle for St. Die was the largest the Division ever experienced.) The Germans were merciless, but the townspeople were great. In the midst of fierce shelling, bombing and the crossfire of countless machine guns, they came out and welcomed us with wine, tears and embraces. We just couldn't get over it. We told them to get back into their cellars, for safety but they ignored us, too intent on celebrating their impending liberation and too eager to show us their appreciation.

"For the second time in twenty years, our brave American friends have come to rescue aged Europe and their godmother, the city of St. Die," said Mayor P. Evrat in a letter to the general in command of the 103rd Division. That was my memory of St. Die fifty years before.

We were now entering St. Die in the direction opposite the way we'd come in 1944. As we neared the town, I couldn't help but cry as I beheld the steep wooded slopes and the beautiful old homes. We had taken this terrain inch by bloody inch back then, or so it seemed. Thank God we'd had such thorough training. Every man had done his part, and many had gone far beyond the call of duty. As vividly as ever, I remembered that buck sergeant we'd called Smitty who ran ahead, throwing hand grenades and clearing the way for the rest of us.

I could not keep my eyes off the tall, old trees. They seemed to be saying, "Don't I know you?" The Germans had used the trees to good advantage, shelling the tops of them, which caused the trunks to burst and rain flaming splinters down on us; a source of many devastating casualties. The splinters fell with lightning speed and often went right through the men they struck. German resistance only got heavier after we passed through St. Die, and the number of our casualties grew dramatically from that point forward.

As the four of us drove into the town, I kept saying, "It's so beautiful." It didn't look at all as I'd remembered it. We had no trouble finding the city hall, and we were delighted when Françoise emerged from her office and greeted us in perfect English. She took us upstairs to a large, well appointed conference room, apologizing for the fact that the mayor couldn't greet us personally, as he was out of town. Françoise introduced us to the deputy mayor, who told us in French (translated by Françoise) how pleased and proud he was to welcome us.

All I had hoped for was the opportunity to meet and videotape some townspeople who had experienced the battle fifty years before, and I had not expected such a gracious, "official" reception. Françoise and the deputy mayor served refreshments and presented us with gifts of posters, three books of their history, and a tape explaining, how, in 1507, the geographers of St. Die were the first to use the word America, in honor of Amerigo Vespucci. In return, I gave

Françoise a cactus pin; the insignia of the 103rd, and for their museum, an original battle map of the area from 1944. I was very tired by now, but who could walk out on this unexpectedly fantastic occurrence? When we brought up our proposed meeting with Pol and Zaig, we learned that the deputy mayor had himself been a slave laborer for seventeen months during the war.

Françoise and the deputy mayor led us outside and down the street, first to a traffic circle built as a monument dedicated to the men of the 103rd Division. It was truly beautiful, with a large green cactus in the center of a patch of yellow flowers. The deputy mayor told us it had been placed there to mark the direction from which the American troops had come. From there, we strolled to the cathedral, which had been bombed during the war, and even now, remained a mere shell of its former self. In the shell, the residents of the town had built a fantastic museum, and as we entered, the curator came out of his office to serve as our personal guide.

Sy at the memorial for the 103rd Infantry Division Monument, St. Die, France

The displays in the museum amazed us. One told the story of the Holocaust. A military section had uniforms and weapons dating back centuries, and included a U.S. Army uniform from World II, complete with a cactus patch on the shoulder. The curator didn't want us to miss a thing, and after a while, the tour seemed a bit overlong. At a point where I didn't think I could go on much longer, Françoise and the curator escorted us into an auditorium, where at least we were able to sit down. They screened three videos of the history of St. Die. I envied Morey, who dozed almost all the way through them. At long last, Françoise took us to the hotel and handed us the keys to our rooms. Before she departed, she told us she had arranged for us to meet Mr. Roland Prieur, superintendent of the American cemeteries in Europe.

So, we got up early next morning and drove the fifty miles to the cemetery near Épinal, where we were to meet Mr. Prieur. I had considered passing up this excursion due to lack of time, but since the remarkable Françoise had set up the meeting, we went and were not sorry. It proved to be one of the highlights of the trip. I cannot describe the wave of emotion that swept over me as some of the 5,225 GI graves came into view, each marked by a white marble Latin cross or Star of David. We found the layout of the cemetery and the architecture of its buildings and monuments stunning; they took our breath away. To see this remote corner of France that would forever be hallowed American ground moved my companions and myself more than I had imagined possible.

An entire wall in the visitors' center was covered in a ceramic tile map of the region, with red arrows displaying the paths taken by the American Divisions that had fought there. It showed the 103rd Division's course all the way to the Brenner Pass in Austria, where they'd ended up at the conclusion of the war in May, 1945. Morey insisted on having me stand next to the large letters that said, "Brenner Pass" for a picture; naturally, I stood in front of the word, "Pass." The insignia of the 103rd appeared right under the word, "Brenner."

Above: The wall in the visitors' center, marking the progress of U.S. forces.

Above: An aerial view of the American Cemetery at Épinal

Outside, the first grave I saw belonged to Sergeant Alfred Neimeyer, who had been my sergeant from the moment I arrived at Camp Claiborne until I joined the medics. I had heard that he'd been killed when his jeep hit a mine-an event happening on the same night I was taken prisoner. My knees buckled with the shock of recognition as I stood before his grave. I began to weep uncontrollably. My life literally passed before my eyes, complete with images of my lovely wife, three children, five grandchildren, successful career; all of this having occurred while "Sarge" lay in a grave far away in a strange land. He used to call me the, "Yard Bird," who never complained as I went about my business. Now, for perhaps the tenth or hundredth time, I muttered, "For the grace of God I could be buried here" and its Yiddish equivalent, "It was "Beshert"." Morey reminded me later that I kept repeating those phrases throughout the day.

Evidently, Mr. Prieur had witnessed such scenes many times before this. With gentle kindness and compassion, he gave me a list of the men from the 103rd who were buried here. I was astounded by the number of my comrades in arms who had died nearby between November 20th and December 1st, 1944. Tired as we were, we wanted to continue on to Nothalden, the place where I'd been captured. But, the driving directions provided by Mr. Prieur seemed complex and circuitous, so once we found ourselves on the road, we decided to head directly for Freiburg, Germany, another main objective of the trip. Try as I might, I couldn't block from my consciousness the memories of how terrible the conditions became after we passed through St. Die.

I had been apprehensive but eager to see Freiburg again, especially the railroad station, because of the traumatic events I'd experienced there. For some of my fellow captives, Freiburg marked the end of our two week march through hell; here the Germans filled a train of boxcars with about half of our contingent for the last stage of the journey to the prison camp. Before my cohort could be loaded onto another train, waves of Allied planes bombed the town, and our guards hustled us away on foot, protecting us from angry civilians. We ended up marching for several more days, again with no food or water and with plenty of whacks on the back and neck with rifle butts. I had been eager to see the railroad station again, but the rainy weather didn't mix well with my exhaustion, and besides, the station was now fenced off for repair. I took one picture from the car and we drove off.

With Freiburg receding in the distance at over 100 miles per hour (true story-we were on the Autobahn, and Morey was loving it!), we headed toward Ludwigsburg, where Stalag V-A had stood. If I'd been nervous and apprehensive before, by now I felt positively fearful. Back home, I'd spoken with other ex-P.O.W.'s who had visited their former prison camps; some had wonderful experiences doing so that liberated them from the burden of the past. In this regard, I hoped my pilgrimage would help to rid me of my constantly recurring nightmares. Others, however, found that such visits brought back to life all too vividly the horror of combat, capture and captivity, and ended up regretting the undertaking. At this point, I just couldn't predict how it would turn out for me.

We reached Ludwigsburg, enjoyed a fine meal, and began to drive around the town in search of the hospital that had once been the Lazarett. Suddenly I

Above: Sy at the Lazarett door.

jumped out of the car while it was still moving and yelled, "That's it!" I recognized the masonry and brick as I ran across the one-way street to the rear entrance of what was left of the World War I stable, around which the modern hospital had been built. The only feature that differed from my memory was a glass door at the main entrance.

As I entered, I asked a passing nurse if this had once been a prison hospital. A big smile crossed her face. Then, she raised an eyebrow, pointed to me and said, "You're not the first one to come back," and walked off. Resa, Morey, and Lois had joined me by this time. I asked Morey to keep his video camera running. The hall was very bright and cheerful, not like fifty years ago. As I got to the end of the hall, I came right to the door of the closet in which I'd been locked for three days and nights with the decaying corpse. It wasn't a closet anymore, but still I clearly recognized it as the site of my most gruesome nightmare. As I talked about it to my companions, Lois remarked that my voice had gotten tinny, and I seemed to be losing control. I was on the verge of tears.

We stood at a window as I tried to explain where things were. About a hundred feet from the door, there had been a barbed wire barrier, and to the left, had been the main entrance to the Lazarett-directly across from the main gate of the Stalag. I pointed out the route I took to The Lady's house, although everything was different now. When we went up the stairs, we were disappointed to find our way blocked by a door chained and locked shut. (We later learned that we had come to the back entrance of a ward for mental patients.) Through a small window in the door, I showed the others the location of the three rooms that had been most important to me-the bandage room, the sleeping quarters I had shared, and the room where we'd amputated Whitey's leg. The combination of frustration, exhilaration and revivified trauma overwhelmed me. I struggled to hold back tears and could speak only in a voice choked by emotion. I wouldn't, "come back to myself" for days.

After my visit to the prison hospital, I found I wasn't in the proper frame of mind to attempt my next goal. But, to my regret, I tried it anyway-a trip to the Archives of the Nazi War Crimes Commission. I wanted to find The Lady. Professor Lawrence Baron of San Diego State University had done some research for me, and had found a woman who resembled The Lady in some important ways, but she turned out not to be the one. He did give me the address of the Archives, which as luck would have it, was right here in Ludwigsburg.

We asked the hotel clerk how to find the building, and he told us there wasn't any such place in town. I asked the manager. He denied any knowledge of the institution or the street on which it was supposed to be. I then called the city administration offices and got the same story. My anger was rising as I asked to speak with the supervisor, who continued with the denial. When I told him I had been a prisoner of war in that city, and that if he didn't help me, I could make some real trouble, he finally gave me directions to where it might be.

The building could not have been in a more obscure location. We found the street-indeed the same one Professor Baron had indicated-but it was in the middle of open, empty fields. Morey decided to follow some tire tracks across a field, and we at last, came to a line of trees, behind which was a building with a security gate and the street address that Professor Baron had given me.

I rang the bell, and a woman asked me through the intercom, in German, who was calling. I identified myself, and she said I could enter, but without my companions. Once inside, I passed a glassed anteroom with three women working away at computer terminals. The rest of the room-in fact the whole place-was somber, and I knew I should have waited until I was feeling better before tackling this situation. I was quite nervous and that must have been obvious to the tall, gaunt man who was coming down the stark slate-gray staircase to meet me. He looked like Gestapo to me, as least as I remembered them from the bad, old days. He said, "My name is Dreisen," with a hiss through his teeth. "Come with me." He had an odd expression on his face, as if he expected me to recognize him, which I didn't. I learned why a few years later when I did actually recognize his name and picture in a newspaper article that appeared in the Detroit Free Press: he was a famous Nazi-hunter, almost as well known around the world as Simon Wiesenthal.

We went upstairs and everything was the same dark slate gray, including the long worktable, which was covered with computer printouts. He asked me what I wanted to see him about, and I told him my story of The Lady. I wanted to know what happened to her, and if she was still alive, I wanted to see her. I showed him my American and German dog tags. Dreisen asked me if I'd been mistreated at the hospital. Thinking it might be easier to get news of The Lady, I lied and said no. He said he'd have to do some checking and that it would take time. He also told me most of the German underground units operating in Germany were in fact run by wives of the generals who had tried to kill Hitler.

Because I felt so poorly, as if I were in a haze, I wasn't at all sure I had communicated very well with Mr. Driesen. There was so much more I wanted to say, but just couldn't. I felt that I needed to go back to the archives and see him again, but I wasn't able to muster the strength. For the next three days, I kept having uncomfortable visions of walking up the painted slate-gray staircase. I felt locked in, almost as if I were suffocating. It was definitely time for us to leave Ludwigsburg.

From Ludwigsburg, we headed to the beautiful old university city of Heidelberg, where we passed a restful couple of days, then back to Paris. Not until then did we manage to reach Pol and Zaig by telephone-a source of some anxiety during the past week. Pol knew where we were staying in Paris, and he said he'd join us three days later. He and Zaig called again the evening before they were to meet us and told us they could stay only a day and a night as they had thirty guests coming to town from Ireland for a music convention.

When the great moment arrived next afternoon, the three of us threw a bear hug on each other, and we all cried like babies. Morey was supposed to have been there to videotape the event, but he hadn't returned on time from his visit to Monet's Garden at Giverny. Resa had tried to fill in, but couldn't insert the battery into the camera, so we have no record of our rendezvous.

Above: Sy, Pol, and Zaig reunited in Paris, 1995.

I told Zaig she was just as beautiful as she'd been in 1945, and that I had something for her. She laughed and said, "I knew you would." It was a large pack of chewing gum, just like I used to send her fifty years ago. The two of them were dressed very smartly-much different from the past. We talked through the afternoon, went out for a wonderful dinner, and finally headed off for bed around eleven o'clock. We planned to meet early the next afternoon; I was so spent that I could only rest until then.

From left to right: Sy, Resa, Pol, and Zaig having dinner in Paris.

Our afternoon together was unforgettable, filled with conversation about all that had taken place in our lives since we'd last seen each other. When we exchanged a few more gifts I was astounded to learn that Zaig had visited San Diego ten years earlier. What a shame I hadn't thought of contacting them sooner! At one point, I asked Pol to tell the story of how, as a slave laborer, he had made schwartzbrot-the ghastly bread that was so important to the P.O.W.'s' diet. His job was to mix the different flours: "One hundred kilos of white flour, one hundred kilos of black flour, fifty kilos of potatoes and fifty kilos of I don't know what. I mixed it. I rolled it, and as I rolled it I threw this stuff in. I didn't know what it was." I said, "Saw dust." Pol continued, "The bread came through a tube, and I would cut it and mark it with a 'k'. I called it 'ka ka.' They exported that bread to all of Germany.

I said, "We were lucky to have it. We got a slice a day with ersatz coffee." I then told them the story about my father giving me the little knife and how I if I cut my bread into small pieces, it would last longer.

Pol mentioned that the slave laborers actually received some money in compensation for their work, only it was ersatz money, just like the coffee. If it didn't have a special stamp on it for food, he couldn't buy anything with it. Then I said, "I'd better go back; I forgot something. All the prisoners of war who worked were supposed to be paid. Thirty marks a day." Pol corrected me-it was thirty pfennigs a day. I responded, "You know, they had a lot of nerve. They never paid me!" Zaig laughed as she said, "You're right. You ought to go back."

It was a wonderful afternoon and it was a shame they had to leave to catch their train. When they'd gone, Resa and I returned to our room and began to pack for the trip home. Except for our reunion with Pol and Zaig, we hadn't had such a great time in Paris. Whenever we'd gone outside, it had rained cats and dogs. Every time we tried to visit a museum, they'd been closed. When we booked a tour of Versailles, we ended up on a city tour instead. And when we took a cab, to the airport, we got thoroughly gypped, again!

On balance, however, we'd found our journey satisfying. I rejoiced that we'd seen St. Die, the cemetery at Épinal and the Lazarett at Ludwigsburg, and regretted that we'd missed Nothalden and not learned anything more of The Lady. I still have my nightmares and flashbacks and suffer other symptoms of Post-traumatic Stress Disorder. I still join the ex-P.O.W. gatherings when I can get a ride. I still wonder whatever happened Tex, Whitey, John Alberti, Bruno Galinski, and even Chris. I knew that Masa Uchimura had died in 2003 of Parkinson's Disease, but what of the rest? What impact did the prisoner-of-war experience have on their lives? How did it all work out for them? Although I guess I'll never know, I take comfort in the thought, as my mother liked to say, that it was all "Beshert"!

Abraham J. Shragge, II

Abraham J. Shragge, II was born and raised in San Francisco and has been a resident of San Diego since 1982. He holds a B.A. in history from U.C. Davis and an M.A. and Ph.D. in Modern U.S. History from the University of California, San Diego. Dr. Shragge spent fourteen years in business (retail scuba diving and commercial real estate) before entering the graduate program at U.C.S.D.. He has taught history at San Diego City College, Mira Costa College and U.C.S.D.. He was a Lecturer in History, Urban Studies and Planning, and Public Service at U.C.S.D.'s Thurgood Marshall College and volunteered curator of the Veterans Museum and Memorial Center in San Diego's Balboa Park. He initiated and coordinated the San Diego Ex-Prisoners of War Oral History program. He is now KDI School of Public Policy and Management in Seoul, Korea. He continues to write on American History.

Samuel "Sy" Brenner

Sy Brenner was born in Montreal, Canada and moved to Detroit, Michigan as an infant. He was granted his United States citizenship while in the U.S. Army boot camp during World War II. Captured by the Nazi's in Southern France, he was on a death march and remanded to Stalag 5A for the remainder of the war. Trained as a medic by the US Army, he was put in charge of the prison hospital, became a Man of Confidence for the prison, and was recruited by the French and German underground. He also had to hide the fact that he was a Jew. After he was married, he moved to California where he and his wife, Resa raised their 3 children. He was a successful Manufacturer's Representative for a major children's clothing line and became a popular speaker with the San Diego School district. Until 1995, he never spoke about his experiences during World War II. He is now very active in San Diego ex-P.O.W. Chapter 1, and his story is part of the P.O.W. exhibit in the Veteran's Memorial Museum in Balboa Park, San Diego. He is a speaker on Post Traumatic Stress Syndrome and has spoken to College Students, Marine and Naval Leadership Classes, and has been made an honorary Top Gun. He has been featured on every local San Diego news stations, on Fox News and various Cable shows. Mr. Brenner is the recipient of 16 medals and awards. He lives in El Cajon, California. Where he remains very active as a volunteer and with making sure that the Prisoners of Wars are not forgotten.